Universal Principles of Interior Design

ROCKPORT

First published in 2022 by Rockport Publishers,
an imprint of The Quarto Group,
100 Cummings Center, Suite 265-D, Beverly, MA 01915, USA.
T (978) 282-9590 F (978) 283-2742 QuartoKnows.com

Rockport Publishers titles are also available at discount for retail, wholesale, promotional, and bulk purchase. For details, contact the Special Sales Manager by email at specialsales@quarto.com or by mail at The Quarto Group, Attn Special Sales Manager, 100 Cummings Center, Suite 265-D, Beverly, MA 01915, USA.

10 9 8 7 6 5 4 3 2 1

ISBN 978-0-7603-7212-8

Digital edition published in 2022
eISBN 978-0-7603-7213-5

Library of Congress Cataloging-in-Publication Data available

Design OverUnder Chris Grimley
Cover Images Patricia Uriquola / Moroso / Photo by Joel Matthias Henry, Doublespace Photography, Bob O'Connor / Kelly Harris Smith.
Back Cover Image Deborah Berke Partners.

Printed in China

Kelly Harris Smith
and Chris Grimley

Universal Principles of Interior Design

100 Ways to Develop
Innovative Ideas, Enhance
Usability, and Design
Effective Solutions

Contents

Introduction

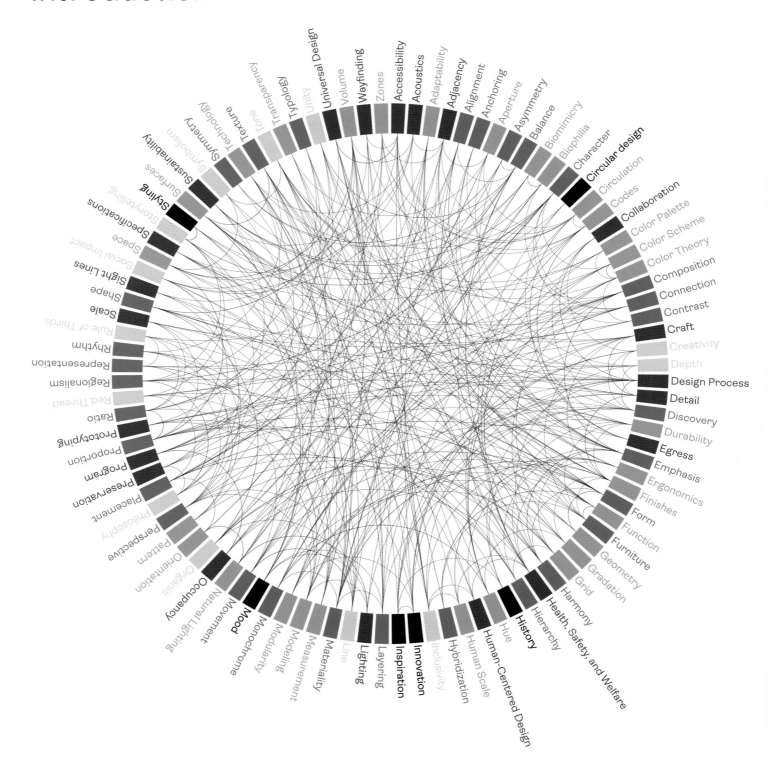

The profession of interior design is a complex, wide-ranging, and creative career. The skills that an interior designer needs are similarly expansive—from the large gestures of space planning, to the finer scales of wall and millwork details, to knowledge of furniture and upholstery techniques, to final styling, artwork selection, and photographic documentation of a project once complete. The kinds of projects that an interior designer is engaged with can range from work of all scales and types, to work in a single, specialized, category. All types of spaces—single homes and dwellings, apartments and condominiums, retail and hospitality environments, commercial and shared office interiors, learning spaces (from early childhood education to universities), arts and performance spaces, health care and assisted living facilities, and hospitals—can be enhanced by the expertise of an interior designer in collaboration with other design and engineering professions.

Universal Principles of Interior Design presents one hundred essential concepts that are critical to the successful visualization and implementation of interior design, pairing explanations of each topic with visual examples of their application in practice.

Universal Principles of Interior Design organizes these one hundred principles of importance to the profession. Arranged alphabetically, these entries function as essential areas of knowledge that a designer—from hobbyist to student to licensed professional—should be aware of. They attempt to cover many of the key intentions, objective and subjective areas of knowledge, and the needs of a professional practitioner. But this is not intended to be a comprehensive guide for everything a designer needs to be cognizant of. Instead, it is meant to be a collection of fundamental concepts that will point toward further exploration and elicit curiosity regardless of expertise level.

Given the range and scale of an interior design practice, it is helpful to step back and discover the larger ideas that link together these principles. To that end, we have indicated these relationships by including "See Also" links that demonstrate the overlaps and connections inherent to them, but also by an additional comprehensive system that broadly places each principle in higher-level categories that demonstrate the importance of the work an interior designer does.

Intention T3hese principles focus on the ways in which an interior designer engages with the philosophy, and impact of our work in the world. This includes ideas about cultural specificity and symbolism, how our persons react to spaces, how we occupy and live within, and our intellectual framing of the conditions of the body in space through inclusive and human-centered design.

Objectivity By looking at research and development within the profession, and the disciplines that surround it, these principles include investigations into how our bodies relate to objects and movement in space, how we interact with and perceive color, how our sense of touch responds to material and texture, and how both natural and artificial light impact our built environment. In addition, issues surrounding sustainability and adaptability, and durability and preservation are anchored in the specialized work of subdisciplines that aim to create a cohesive and successful project.

Subjectivity These principles engage with the more elusive elements that make a design complete—principles that operate in the space between intention and technology. Concepts like harmony, balance, symmetry, and their counterparts are considered highly subjective and often highly debated areas of design discourse. These principles, concerned with contentious and complex questions of style, taste, beauty, the "proper" use of materials, furniture, and lighting will always elicit strong opinions and emotions. Navigating these opinions is often complicated by current trends, yet there are lessons to be learned from precedents and history.

Professional These principles are more technical, and often have liability implications, as they are the areas of expertise that involve life safety, coordination with other consultants, standards, specifications, and licensing.

Inspiration As a designer, how, where, and to whom do you look to stay curious, keep abreast of best practices, trends, and developments in the profession, and find the creative spark needed to begin a project? These principles are framed around the media and concepts that have been useful to us as designers in practice. For many, the wealth of magazines, media channels, and websites dedicated to the profession are a constant source of inspiration. Developing a curated collection of inspirations to turn to that is consistently revisited with a discerning eye is a critical aspect of being a design professional.

This book is for interior design students, practitioners, and educators, as well as others who seek to broaden and improve their understanding of and expertise in interior design. We hope that it encourages further investigation into this remarkable and creative field, and opens eyes and minds to the possibilities of a satisfying design practice. Regardless of expertise, we hope this book finds a place in your library, and continues to prompt curiosity and inspiration for everyone.

01 Accessibility

Design that accommodates and adapts for use by people
with disabilities.

See Also
Circulation
Ergonomics
Inclusivity
Universal Design

Designers, developers, and building owners are responsible for
ensuring that buildings and spaces are accessible to everyone. This
includes, but is not limited to, anyone with a mobility or ambulatory
impairment, such as wheelchair users, people with strollers, people
with vision or hearing impairments, and older adults.

Accessibility is an important part of any design project and is often
required by law before a certificate of occupancy can be granted.
Standards and guidelines are typically defined by national, state, or
provincial, and local jurisdictions and as such can vary depending
on the type of project. It is advised that you check with the local
municipality on accessibility requirements prior to beginning your
design. When necessary, an accessibility code consultant can perform
an audit and assist designers in understanding the requirements for
each project.

While the needs of people with disabilities are different, every design
project should consider accessibility. By planning for and adhering to
accessibility guidelines, it's possible to both design beautiful spaces
and meet the needs of those with disabilities.

There are multiple ways in which accessibility can be an integral part
of the design process.

Space
Open, unimpeded space, wider
hallways, and enlarged door
openings contribute to the ease
of use by someone with a dis-
ability. The turning radius of a
wheelchair (5'-0" or 1.5m) must
always be considered. Broader
entryways to buildings, accessible emergency exits, and larger
bathroom cubicles are a result
of these design modifications.

Vertical Access
Incorporating ramps, lifts,
and elevators into the building
design is advised as stepped
conditions are considerably
more difficult if not impossible
for disabled people to navigate.
In addition, visible, audible,
and tactile displays are required
at and near elevators to allow
wheelchair users to move independently within the building.

Surfaces
Smooth floors make it possible
for people in wheelchairs or
walkers to navigate effectively,
and the addition of handrails,
grab bars, and tactile indicators
for changes in surfaces and
material is suggested.

Heights and Location
The current standard heights
of kitchen counters and work
surfaces are dangerously high
and should be lowered. Putting
hot objects like kettles or pots
above head height means there
is an increased risk for spills or
burns. Desk systems should be
adjustable in both width and
height to accommodate wheelchair users. Lowering bathroom
counters and storage locations
to be more reachable, allowing
for space under counters, and
lowering the position of light
switches and outlets are all
needed modifications when
designing with accessibility.

In this Boston residence, the architect Chris Greenawalt designed a wheelchair-friendly apartment by adding low counters and accessible under-counter space.

Technology

The increasing ubiquity of automatic door openers, smart technology, interactive monitors, smart appliances, and security systems reduces the need for touch and grip surfaces, and allows users to set temperature on thermostats, prepare meals, and schedule laundry.

02 Acoustics

The qualities of a space that reflect or absorb sound waves.

See Also
Adjacency
Emphasis
Surface
Volume

Further Reading
Baux, *The Book of Acoustics Making People Happy at Work*, (Vulkan, 2021). www.baux.com/book-of-acoustics/.

The goal of acoustic design is to serve the space's intended function and the users', collective needs. Understanding how sound works is key to creating an environment that is supportive of how the space functions. When a sound wave is produced, it travels and bounces off the reflective surfaces it comes in contact with. The amount of time it takes (in seconds) for that sound energy to dissipate is called "reverberation time" (RT).

The reverberation of a sound wave is affected by all surfaces and contents within a room, including the flooring, furniture, window treatments, and even people. In a space containing hard and reflective walls, floors, and ceilings, sound waves bounce around the room multiple times before they become inaudible, resulting in an echoey room.

Lengthy reverberation times allow sounds to build up and conflict with one another. Ideal reverberation times can vary based on how the space is used; however, a range from around 0.6 to 0.8 seconds is ideal for an office space. Short RTs (under 1 second) are preferable for high-quality intelligibility in private offices, meeting rooms, and classrooms.

Designers can't always control the sound that takes place in a space, but they can specify materials and products that absorb, block, cover, or diffuse sound, which reduce reverberation time to an acoustically comfortable range.

Notre Dame cathedral in Paris was damaged by fire in 2019. While the cathedral is being rebuilt, researchers are attempting to restore the medieval church's reverberant acoustics.

The Noise Reduction Coefficient (NRC) is a value ranging from 0.0 to 1.0 that measures sound-absorption performance of materials.

Materials and Their NRCs

Reflective		
	Glass	0.03
	Metals	0.025
	Ceramics, Stone	0.01–0.02
	Concrete	0.03
	Plastered Masonry	0.25

Absorptive		
	Textile	Varies on product
	Glass Wool	0.68
	Rock Wool	0.72
	Acoustic Foams	0.50
	Wood Fiber	0.57
	Cork	0.20-0.70

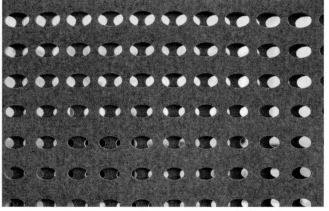

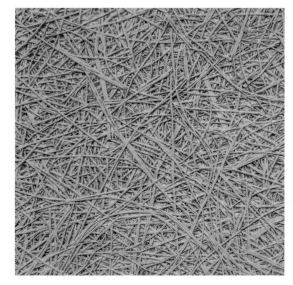

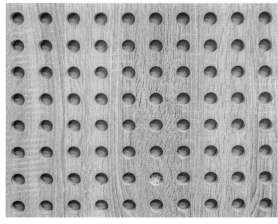

Acoustic materials cork, felt, wood fiber panel, and perforated wood.

03 Adaptability

Design solutions that accommodate change.

See Also
Design Process
Discovery
Innovation
Modularity

Adaptability in interior design is the capacity of a space or environment to accommodate evolving demands and maximize value throughout its intended use. This strategy embodies structural, spatial, and service strategies that allow for alterations over time.

The word *adapt* appears in fourteenth-century Latin as *optus*, meaning "suited, fitted." When it appeared in English in the 1600s, it was defined as "to fit something for some purpose."

Flexible interiors are different for various types of spaces and users. In retail, inventory inevitably changes every season; companies may outgrow their offices or have staffing changes that necessitate change. In a home, the sudden need to work from home or educate a child necessitates different spatial uses.

By prioritizing flexibility, it is possible to design with change from the early phases of a project so the space will easily adapt when new opportunities or challenges occur. With a flexible design, you can adapt and support shifting technology requirements and work styles as needed.

Open floor plans can accommodate changes in the future, and many new urban residential buildings are being developed with "flex spaces" within each unit that can transform into a home gym, home office, kids' playroom, or guest bedroom.

Multifunctional furnishings include adjustable-height desks, divider screens or wall panels that can be easily moved, lounge furniture on casters, collapsible conference tables, and modular seating arrangements that allow quick transformation in small spaces.

Rooms can be easily rearranged with movable furniture. The same space can be reconfigured into multiple uses

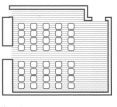

Lecture

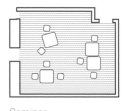

Seminar

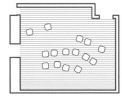

Studio

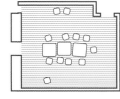

Workshop

Verb, a furniture collection by Steelcase, is designed to support a range of teaching styles and classroom environments with mobile tables, whiteboards, adjustable teaching lecturns, and desk stations.

Barcelona-based BONBA Studio incorporated a desk, shelves, and even lighting into the back of this bed's headboard to accommodate for space restrictions. The space can easily be adapted for sleeping, working, or studying.

04 Adjacency

The system for determining how spaces relate to each other.

See Also
Design Process
Discovery
Program
Zones

There are many ways to develop plans that allow for natural pairings of spaces according to their spatial relationship.

In the predesign phase, space planning is critical to ensure that the flow of a space is maximized and that routes are efficient. This phase is analytical and iterative. Based on conversations with a client or client group, there are several methods that can be used to develop adjacencies. The process is based on trial and error—some elements that appear to have requirements that they be near each other may not end up together based on this exercise.

There are several ways to assess adjacency needs, and all are affected by the physical space of a project. A list of these needs can include the following working needs, adjacency to natural light, acoustic qualities, access to specialized equipment or water, privacy, accessibility or sustainability needs, and maintenance.

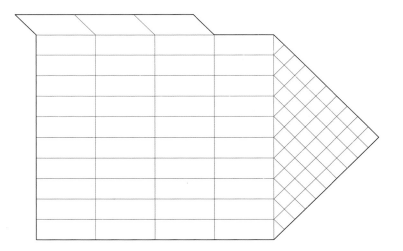

Adjacency Matrix
A format that takes all of the parts of a program and stacks them vertically. A diagrid then connects them together. The designer assigns levels of connection (color dots or numbers) where the programs meet. This allows for quick visualization of adjacency needs.

Bubble Diagrams

A series of quick sketches—usually drawn by hand—that lay out visually the results of the adjacency matrix. Many options should be tested and evaluated; the most successful of which are then brought forward to the next phase of plan development.

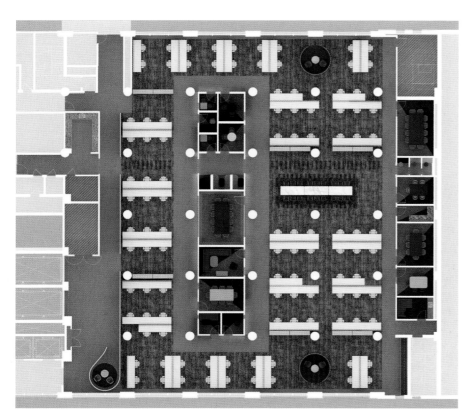

Sketch Plans

Using the the bubble diagram alongside with space requirements, sketches (with or without furniture) and drawings begin to test the needs within the confines of the project.

05 Alignment

The arrangement of elements along a line.

See Also
Balance
Emphasis
Grid
Line

Alignment is the technique by which a designer organizes movement through a space by using visual cues, place cabinets in an elevation, or the matches in a wood veneer. Cabinets and finish carpentry are sure of the most impactful elements in a design. They are also the most meticulous when coordinating with adjacent walls and finishes. In this, alignment is key. Thinking spatially, vertical and horizontal lines that do not align will look careless and disorganized.

Other elements with vertical and horizontal lines provide opportunities for using alignment as a tool for symmetry, or using misalignment as a method of destabilizing a design. Shelves, windows, artwork, as well as wall- or ceiling-mounted lights are all ways in which alignment can help organize a space.

Furniture and other objects don't need to be positioned at right angles to walls. If a space is big enough, principles of asymmetrical arrangement can be used to align objects so that they appear dynamic and compositionally at odds with the geometry of the room.

Well-coordinated alignments in utilitarian spaces emphasize usability and function.

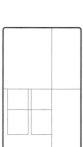

The asymmetrical arrangement and alignment of furniture in MIT's Media Lab's social spaces contributes to a dynamic space.

Light fixtures by RBW are carefully arranged over tables to provide order and function in this café.

05 Alignment   19

06 Anchoring

The use of an element to ground or weigh down a space.

See Also
Composition
Emphasis
Form
Layering

An anchoring element is an object or surface that can be the catalyst for the design of a room or a series of connected spaces. By having an outsized impact on the overall composition, the anchor element provides cues around which other design decisions can be further developed.

An anchor element can take the form of many materials and objects, whether it is an important work of art, a heavier (darker) material on a surface, or an opening that through absence makes its presence felt. Anchoring elements should provide the focal point for a space, and should not be overwhelmed by the placement of competing adjacent objects. The lighting of an anchor object is critical to the composition, and intense spotlighting can further enhance its impact.

Examples of anchoring elements includes

A fireplace with surrounding symmetrical built-in shelving provides an anchoring point in this living room.

Objects
A painting, photograph, sculpture, or light installation.

Furniture
A large table that dominates a room, an arrangement of furniture or light fixtures in a space.

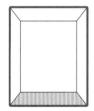

Horizontal Surfaces
A darker floor that draws the eye down or an area rug on a lighter surface.

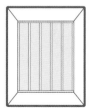

Vertical Surfaces
Elevating a wall through bold use of paint, textile, or wood paneling.

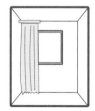

Heavy Textiles
Framing a window with excessive drapery or using acoustic wall products.

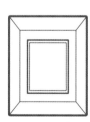

Apertures
Somewhat counter-intuitive, a large window or opening can, through the absence of surface, act as the center of interest in a space.

The large patterned carpet acts as an anchor in this hotel room and ties the space together. Without floor covering, furniture pieces can appear to be floating and disconnected.

Large-scale graphic wall covering visually anchors this long, linear lounge space in the Slack headquarters designed by Studio O+A.

07 Aperture

An opening or gap in a surface.

See Also
Adjacency
Circulation
Movement
Natural Lighting

Apertures are the moments in a design where openings occur, where light passes through glass, and how air circulates in a space. Traditionally thought of as having functional value, a door to get into another space (or to close off access), a window to allow light and exterior environments into the space, or empty openings in both horizontal or vertical surfaces allow for visual access to other spaces.

The depth and material of an aperture can affect the perception of what is beyond an opening. A regular stud wall is too slight to elicit a physical response when you pass through it, but a knife edge detail or a much thicker wall assembly registers with the body's movement.

Apertures in exterior walls were historically tied to climatic conditions, as an opening in a wall compromised the heating or cooling necessary. Deep apertures for daylight modulate the way light enters a room, and can provide protection and shade on a bright day. Prior to the invention of glazing and heat-gain protection, apertures were minimized to keep heat out, and wall thickness was integral to staying cool or moderating the interior temperature.

In addition to wall openings, openings in ceilings and floors can create dramatic double-height spaces and skylit conditions. These are just some of the creative ways to use the additional surfaces of a project, and allow for visual and aural connection to adjacent spaces.

A deep threshold connects two spaces in Minni, a children's design studio in Boston, Massachusetts.

In the painting *Interior of the Pantheon, Rome,* by Giovanni Paulo Panini c. 1734, highlights central oculus in its coffered dome, which acts the main source of light for the ancient temple.

The skylight at the MIT Chapel in Cambridge provides diffuse light over the alter, highlighting the undulating brick interior walls.

08 Asymmetry

The absence of symmetry.

See Also
Balance
Emphasis
Placement
Symmetry

While symmetry denotes regularity by mirroring or reflecting around a central axis, an asymmetrical design strategy is more informal, allowing elements to be arranged freely in space. Multiple objects, mismatched furnishings, and odd numbers of elements can work together to form a creative composition/design/arrangement.

This strategy does not necessarily mean that the room appears unbalanced. The lack of a formal organizing strategy has the benefit of diversifying the composition, and showing naturalness and ways of movement within a space. Lounges and living rooms, in particular, are great for these layouts as they encourage interactions at both the scale of the room and for more intimate moments. In work environments, asymmetrical designs offer spaces for informal meetings and places for focused work.

Asymmetry is often found in furniture, pattern, textile design, and art. In Japanese culture, there are several terms that embrace asymmetry in practice. *Hacho* means intentional unevenness or asymmetrical balance. *Ma* is the emptiness and space around an object, often found in art or music. *Kabuku* means to lean, or to be unusual or out of the ordinary. *Ikenobo* is the Buddhist practice of arranging standing flowers asymmetrically to represent natural forms.

Charles and Ray Eames's asymmetrical La Chaise lounge (1948; reissued in 1996 by Vitra) was designed for the Museum of Modern Art. Difficulties in production made it impossible to build until Vitra was able to fabricate it in 1996.

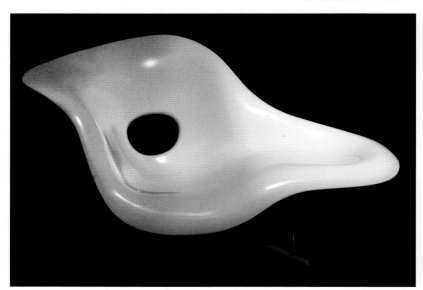

Modular furniture, like Turnstone's Campfire Lounge System, is easier to arrange in asymmetrical designs.

In their revamp of Phillipe Starck's iconic Paramount Hotel in New York, the Meyer Davis design retains some of the original's sense of asymmetrical layout, but through placement of furniture and use of light.

09 Balance

The aesthetically pleasing arrangement of elements within a space.

See Also
Asymmetry
Harmony
Hierarchy
Symmetry
Unity

Visual balance is based on equal distribution of elements, and is an important principle and goal for interior designers. Most spaces require visual balance, which can be achieved by distributing the visual weight of objects/elements within a space to achieve a feeling of equilibrium. There are three types of balance in interior design symmetrical, asymmetrical, and radial.

Helpful Advice
It's important to not only design placement of furniture and elements in plan, but to also consider the height and visual weight of these elements in elevation or in three dimensions to understand the full impact of those objects placed in a space. Similarly, be careful not to underestimate the visual weight of patterning or color in accessories, plants, pillows, and decorative items, which may not always be included in initial design drawings.

Meticulous design details and colorful frieze frame the reception area at the Line Hotel DC in Washington, D.C. by INC Architecture + Design.

Symmetrical Balance
Also referred to as "formal balance," symmetrical balance is most pleasing to the eye. By dividing a room into equal sides or halves, or along a central axis, symmetry can be achieved by placing matching elements on both sides of the room to mirror each other. One example is placing a pair of sofas across a table from each other with matching side tables and lamps. This type of balance is commonly practiced in traditional spaces, easy to achieve in square rooms, and can have a calming effect, but often comes across as bland, static, or monotonous. Symmetrical balance can also be influenced by the use of color or pattern, millwork, smaller fixtures, and decor.

The House of Wine in Znojmo, Czech Republic, designed by Chybik + Kristof, arranges curved volumes clad in dark plywood that divide the interior into several smaller seating areas.

Asymmetrical Balance

Asymmetrical balance is often practiced in modern or contemporary interiors, and balances the visual weight of objects, lines, colors, and textures without exact duplication from one side of the room to the other side. Rather than repeating elements on each side of a central axis, it balances a variety of elements working together (such as balancing a sofa with two lounge chairs on either side of an axis). Various objects can be added to a room to achieve asymmetrical balance. Sometimes an odd number of objects is purposefully placed in order to achieve asymmetry in the space. This type of balance may be visually more complex and interesting, but also more difficult to achieve because it is not as ordered as symmetrical balance, proportional objects, or furniture.

Radial Balance

In radial balance, objects are arranged radially in a circular manner around a central focal point. Less commonly used, radial balance works with the presence of curved structures, like staircases, circular dining tables, or large, round light fixtures. Repetitions of curves, colors, and patterns are common in radial balance. Positioning a round table with a circular light fixture above and with chairs equally arranged around the table is one way to achieve radial balance.

As an unbalanced space can be uncomfortable, an interior designer's goal is to create a feeling of balance and aesthetic equilibrium for the user(s). Any combination of these types of balance are possible within a home, office, or other spaces.

In radial balance, the distributed arrangement of items radiates around a central point, extending outward or inward. In this case a lectern at the European parliament hemicycle in Strasbourg, France is the focal point.

10 Biomimicry

The emulation of natural biological designs or processes.

See Also
Biophilia
Materiality
Sustainability
Technology

The term *biomimicry* is derived from the ancient Greek words *bios* (meaning life) and *mimesis* (meaning imitation); in other words, something that imitates life.

In 1982, Janine Benyus—known as the founder of the movement—defined biomimicry as a "new science that provides innovative and sustainable solutions for industry and research development." For example, Leonardo da Vinci's 1488 studies of birds and his drawings for the "Design for a Flying Machine" are early examples of biomimicry's influence on design. Throughout history, there have been numerous design movements and designers that look to nature for influence and inspiration.

Biomimicry also drives material innovation, whether it is the technology that allows growable forms (mycelium bricks, for example) or bioluminescence, seating that is shaped like smooth pebbles, hexagonal wall tiles, or patterned textiles that take inspiration from nature and its forms.

The preserved remains of Hadrian's Villa in Tivoli, Italy, illustrate that ancient Roman dwellings (and those from other early civilizations) were designed to function harmoniously with nature and the local environment.

The Shanghai Natural History Museum by Perkins&Will integrates nature and architecture, from the overall site plan to the unique cell-structured walls of the facade and interior atrium, to the use of natural materials and local resources.

Designed by Jason F. McLennan, founder of the Living Product Challenge, the Lichen flooring collection for Mohawk Group is "inspired by assemblages of multi-hued, multitextured lichens and their regenerative role in our ecosystem and is on the path to give more resources back to the environment than it uses during its entire life cycle."

11 Biophilia

The innate biological connection of humans to nature.

See Also
Biomimicry
Materiality
Organic
Sustainability

Further Reading
William Browning, Joseph Clancy, and Catherine Ryan. "14 Patterns of Biophilic Design Improving Health & Well-Being in the Built Environment."
www.terrapinbright-green.com/reports/14-patterns/

Popularized by psychoanalyst Erich Fromm in the 1960s, the word *biophilia* (from *bio*, meaning "life," and *philia*, meaning "friendly feeling toward") describes our innate biological drive for self-preservation. Biophilic design is believed to improve psychological and physiological health by decreasing stress, decreasing recovery time from illness or injury, and improving creativity and productivity. In the workplace, this can also lead to fewer employee sick days, which saves companies funds annually.

Many designers assume that adding plants is all that is needed, but biophilic design is most successful as a multisensory experience. For example, designing with a combination of natural elements—a green moss wall in an office, an abundance of large planters, natural light, windows to bring the outdoors in, water elements (such as fountains), and even sounds and scents of nature—can improve living conditions.

Examples of biophilic design include

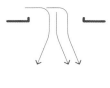

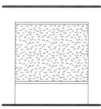

Light
Maximizing natural light, adding lighting systems that change throughout the day to mimic circadian rhythm, increases visual comfort.

Plants
Adding green walls, inserting planters, connecting to the outdoors through rooftop gardens and outdoor dining, and moving work outdoors amid seasonal vegetation.

Air
Thermal and airflow variability impacts comfort, well-being, and productivity, and improves concentration.

Water
The presence of water features, such as fountains, reduces stress, provides feelings of tranquility, and lowers heart rate and blood pressure.

Sound and Smell
Sounds and scents of nature—breezes, leaves rustling, water babbling, birds chirping, and the fragrance of flowers and trees. Atmospheres can be simulated with billowing fabric that moves with the breeze, reflections of light or water on a surface, or mechanically released oils or scents.

A living wall and natural materials provide a tranquil sanctuary from college life in this nook at the refurbished Smith Campus Center at Harvard University in Cambridge, Massachusetts.

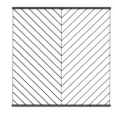

Materials

Natural materials, highlighting wood grain and veining of stone, wool, cork, and leather. The exclusion of materials with perceived toxicity, such as plastics, vinyls, and so on.

Art and Patterns

When all else fails, adding art with nature themes or colors found in nature can help increase the biophilic elements in a space. The same goes for patterns. Our brain associates the use of biophilia in patterns and fractals in nature-based designs with living things.

The Farnsworth House, 1951, by Ludwig Mies van der Rohe, utilizes subtle wood grain as an organizing device and travertine as an anchor material, while transparent glass and sheer curtains highlight the relationship of interior to exterior, and to the river beyond.

12 Character

The visual and physical features that contribute to the appearance of a space.

See Also
Color Scheme
Mood
Regionalism
Storytelling

The tone that is perceived upon entering a room reflects the character of a space. That character can be existing, such as in the case of historic elements or as-found conditions at a project or site, or evolve independently as part of the discussion with a client.

Character is closely aligned with a project's design strategy to help clarify what makes a solution distinctive and compelling. It is occasionally referred to as *style*, but that terminology has a reductive quality based on a narrow selection of objects for a design based on characteristics, rather than on an eclectic or heterogeneous combination of objects and surfaces that create a cohesive whole.

In the process of design, character evolves with the existing conditions of a project. Design strategies can be developed to enhance the space with similar harmonious elements, or juxtapose elements by working in opposition to the character to create a design that revels in its independence.

A graphic wood-screened ceiling adds rich tones and character to the restaurant at the Blackbird Hotel in Bandung, Indonesia.

The lobby of the Standard Hotel and Lido Spa in Miami, Florida, conceived by Shawn Hausman Design, mixes Art Deco-inspired stained glass windows and furniture with a serene, airy, and beach inspired atmosphere. The hotel also incorporates their own signature scent into the ventilation to add to the experience.

A chair from Patricia Urquiola's Lilo Collection for Moroso is inspired by a mix of Scandinavian style, mid-century modernist flair, and the work of Italian designer Achille Castiglioni, who Urquiola apprenticed with early in her career.

13 Circular Design

An economic approach to design that eliminates waste, increases the lifespan of products, and regenerates materials.

See Also
Adjacency
Durability
Health, Safety, and Welfare
Sustainability

Construction debris accounts for a staggering fifty percent of the solid waste generated each year in the U.S. As landfill sites accumulate, chemicals from waste materials that do not biodegrade can enter our food and water supply chains, and thus endanger the health of humans, and harm the land and bodies of water. Conceived by Ellen MacArthur in 2010, circular design is an interconnected alternative to traditional recycling. Also known as a "circular economy," circular design refers to an economic system that aims to eliminate waste and reduce consumption by reusing, repairing, and recycling to create a potentially closed-loop system.

The core principles of circular design include designing out, eliminating, or reducing waste and pollution; improving productivity and durability, allowing for longer use of products and materials; and supporting the regeneration of natural systems. For an interior designer, this means choosing reclaimed textiles and furniture pieces, and carefully evaluating the composition of floor and wall products. In addition, consideration of the life cycle of the product, where and how it will be recycled, and how repurposing components will be paid for is critical to circular design's success.

Examples of industries that are adopting a circular design system include subscription-based furniture companies, textile manufacturers that grind up and refiberize waste material to make new products, or flooring companies that have programs that take back their carpet tiles after use.

The ultimate goal of developing a circular economy approach within a design is to reduce long-term costs, become resource efficient, generate revenue through material reuse, and have an environmental impact.

Helpful Advice
According to the Ellen MacArthur Foundation, "waste and pollution are not accidents, but the consequences are made at the design stage, where 80 percent of environmental impacts are decided."

Digital Bloom 2.0, an upholstery and panel textile by HBF Textiles, contains one hundred percent recycled content and is also one hundred percent biodegradable with third-party certifications from SCS Indoor Advantage, NSF, and Clean Impact Textiles.

Take   Make   Dispose

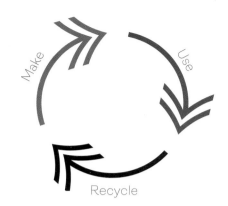

Make   Use   Recycle

Linear Economy   Circular Economy

Normann Copenhagen's
Bit Stool Collection
(2021) uses one hun-
dred percent recycled
household and industrial
plastic.

14 Circulation

The method by which users move through space.

See Also
Adjacency
Codes
Egress
Zones

When we move through space, we use our senses to determine the most efficient route from A to B. This ease of movement, or circulation, is critical to conceptually planning interior space, and to ensuring that levels of comfort and safety are met. There are several ways in which circulation can affect a design, both along a route and vertically.

Horizontal Circulation Hallways, entries, and exits, ways through a room. Affected by placement of furniture and width dictated by code.

Vertical Circulation Stairs, escalators, and elevators.

Circulation is also closely connected to the program of a space—there is more circulation required in a hotel than a private residence, and the occupancy load will dictate the width that corridors and hallways will be. Efficient circulation is critical to designing a project, and is an important factor in determining the total usable area of a project. This is especially important when performing initial programming studies on a commercial space.

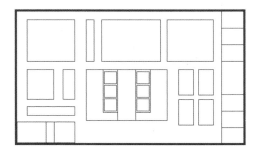

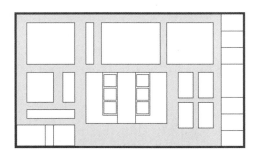

Circulation Area
The space in a plan that is not programmed or programmable, in square feet/square meters.

Circulation Factor
The circulation area divided by the usable square feet/meters.

Circulation Multiplier
The net area divided by the circulation area.

Circulation and program are intertwined. Stairs and elevators, when carefully considered, can have an impact on the experience of a space.

15 Codes

A collection of regulations adopted by a city to govern the construction of buildings and interiors.

See Also
Accessibility
Egress
Health, Safety, and Welfare

Building codes are the regulatory and legal rules that designers must follow to ensure the safety and durability of a building or space. There is a layered structure to how codes apply, moving from the national, down to regional and local variations. It is a designer's responsibility to ensure that their plans are in compliance with the applicable regulations in their area. Building departments are charged with the enforcement of codes and will review all plans prior to issuing a permit. Understanding the structure of codes is important, many sections overlap, and there are cross references throughout that can be complex.

Why Building Codes Matter
The establishment of a baseline set of rules for a design ensure that a building or interior is safe to occupy. Examples include rules that determine the size of stairs, the composition of walls for fire ratings, the appropriate use of materials on surfaces, and how much energy a building may use.

These regulations set out the proper width for doors and hallways, minimum heights for rooms, clearances for vertical circulation, and the many standards that materials must conform to. A separate document, the International Residential Code, applies to one- and two-family dwellings and townhouses not more than three stories above grade. Codes are updated frequently, so the designer should remain up to date with current standards.

In most building codes, there are sections that interior designers should be especially knowledgeable about, including sections on interior finishes, fire and smoke protection, means of egress, accessibility, interior environments, and energy efficiency.

The Impact of the Americans with Disabilities Act. Passed in 1990 the Americans with Disabilities Act (ADA) provides a legal framework for ensuring that spaces are accessible for all people. It outlines dimensional standards for widths of corridors, mounting heights for fixtures and counters, visual and tactile access standards, among many other elements. It is important to note that building codes do not necessarily encompass rules set out in the ADA, and it is the designer's responsibility to talk with the appropriate permitting offices to ensure compliance.

Many projects require the placement of exit signs indicating the nearest means of egress, as in the Kilachand Center at Boston University, which was designed by Payette.

The Kiasma Museum in Helsinki, Finland, incorporates an elegant ramp to adhere to local building codes.

16 Collaboration

The method of working with other professionals.

See Also
Creativity
Design Process
Inspiration

Collaboration refers to the process of design teams working together to achieve a common goal or result. Whether it's working closely with the client, the contractor, or an external consultant during the design process, collaboration is an important part of all stages of interior design projects.

In architecture and interior design, there are many types of consultants that may be hired to work on a project, depending on scale and type. A consultant is typically a licensed professional in a particular field. While there are no existing set standards for engaging consultants for an interior project, hiring a consultant depends on the scope of the project.

Collaboration is also critical in design education. Black Mountain College, an experimental college in North Carolina modeled on the Staatliches Bauhaus in Germany, was founded in the 1930s as a place for artistic collaboration, where visual artists, designers, and poets were encouraged to work together across disciplines, expanding ideas of what constituted a design education.

As in any other creative industry, there are other collaborations in the design profession where manufacturers work with external designers to develop collections of furniture, textiles, flooring, or lighting. There is added value when the designer brings a fresh perspective to the process, and together the company and the designs can reach a larger audience through the partnership.

Types of Consultants
Acoustic Engineer
Art Consultant
Code Consultant
Color Specialist
Electrical Engineer
Fire Protection Engineer
Furniture Consultant
Kitchen Consultant
Landscape Architect
Lighting Consultant
Mechanical Engineer
Plumbing Engineer
Wayfinding Consultant
Sustainability Consultant
Structural Engineer

The increasing use of real-time software has made the process of collaboration, coordination, and construction more efficient. Products such as Bluebeam's Revu collect all documents for the project, and allow for instant communication among teams and stakeholders.

In 2017, Danish brand HAY collaborated with IKEA on the YPPERLIG collection, a line of furniture and accessories.

Buckminster Fuller and students of Black Mountain College assemble a geodesic dome in 1948.

17 Color Palette

The use of a range of colors in an interior space.

See Also
Color Theory
Hue
Monochrome
Tone

Helpful Advice
There are several online tools to help begin a color palette. Sherwin Williams has "ColorSnap," snapyourcolors.com, and Glidden and PPG developed "Visualize Color," www.visualizecolor.com

Any discussion of the use of color in a design setting is sure to elicit strong opinions from a number of sources—how do you start; what is the point of color choices when rules are made to be broken; no one sees color the same, so why should we bother? There are a number of solutions to working with color that are important to the interior design process. The next principles on color address some of the concerns that the wide range of knowledge in the field of color have researched, tested, and tried to quantify. Ideally, the designer starts with color theory, which leads to the developments of a color direction or scheme, which is finally refined into a color palette.

Once a direction for a color strategy has been decided on, the conversation moves to the idea of a specific color palette. This is the fine-tuned exploration of a specific range of colors selected from an agreed-upon strategy.

For example, as a designer you have chosen an analogous color scheme as the basis of your project. If the base color is a pale blue, then the next iteration will be the selection of a specific hue of blue to begin assembling your palette.

Other considerations include the texture of objects you choose, their glossiness (reflectivity) or absorptive materiality, and how much additional light they bleed into an environment. For instance, a highly reflective blue wall will throw a blue-toned color to adjacent, lighter surfaces. This can be used to great effect when thinking of a series of interiors as a whole.

Dark green and red tones mix with subtle muted neutrals on furniture, flooring, and walls in a lounge space.

Kuchar chose a series
of muted hues for this
furniture showroom in
Chicago.

18 Color Scheme

A particular combination of colors.

See Also
Color Theory
Hue
Monochrome
Tone

Further Reading
Diana Hathaway Timmons, "60-30-10 Color Rule How to Use It, and How to Break It," The Spruce, updated April 8, 2021, www.thespruce.com/timeless-color-rule-797859.

A color scheme is a general system for determining how the balance of various hues will interact. As a system, it is separate from specific types of materials that have applied or integral colors in them. In practical applications, color schemes define a direction for the designer to further develop more specific color palettes. For example, a design might call for a monochromatic color scheme. This could take a variety of color directions that would be further explored in the application of a palette (a neutral set of blues, a dark collection of greys), which would then lead to the development of these colors in materials.

Color schemes can be as simple as the one mentioned above, or can begin to contain several colors and color temperatures that can be tested against the metrics of color balance. In color balance, an aesthetic judgement is made toward the harmonious mix and percentages of color. In general, the 60-30-10 Color Rule can be used as a base, but rules are meant to be broken. A confident designer can apply an unexpected mix of colors that surprises and delights.

Color schemes (and opinions about them) are highly ephemeral, and options about what schemes are popular and in fashion change quickly. But what is interior design but a temporal fascination?

Color schemes can encompass the entire project, be room-based, or zoned to just a portion of a project. Even though there are rules in place, the talent in the designer lies in breaking them.

The 60-30-10 Rule
A good rule of thumb is to develop a color scheme in which 60 percent of the space is in a dominant color—this can be walls, furniture, or other objects; 30 percent is reserved for a secondary color—this is usually smaller pieces of furniture or treatments; while the remaining 10 percent is an accent color.

Universal Principles of Interior Design

The Israeli artist Yaacov Agam's multicolored and kinetic installation *Salon Agam* at the Centre Pompidou in Paris, France. The room was originally meant to be set at the entrance of the French presidential private apartments in the Palais de l'Élysée.

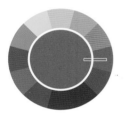

Monochromatic
Uses a single color in a variety of saturations and lightnesses to unify a scheme.

Analogous
Uses colors directly adjacent to the chosen color. The prime color serves as the dominant color in the scheme.

Complementary
High-contrast scheme developed by pairing the chosen color with that directly opposite on the color wheel.

Split Complementary
Variation on the complementary scheme that pairs the chosen color with two adjacent colors.

Triadic

Uses colors equally spaced around the color wheel. Produces high-contrast schemes.

Tetradic
Uses two complementary color pairs. Proportions of colors must be chosen carefully to maintain balance.

19 Color Theory

A set of rules or guiding principles that relate to how hues interact in a space.

See Also
Color Scheme
Hue
Monochrome
Tone

Further Reading
Hella Jongerius, *I Don't Have a Favourite Colour*. (gestalten, 2016).

Many attempts have been made to establish methodologies to evaluate the advantages of certain color combinations. Very early on, color wheels or color spheres were engaged to visually communicate the associations and range of colors, and their relationships to each other. In his *Opticks* of 1704, Isaac Newton split white light into seven colors—orange, yellow, green, blue, indigo, violet, and red—arranged on a disk in proportionate slices such that the spinning of the disk would result in the color white. Newton's objectification of color into a mathematically understandable system allowed for quantifiable experimentation.

Over time, color theory has evolved into several strategies and empirical ways to relate colors to each other.

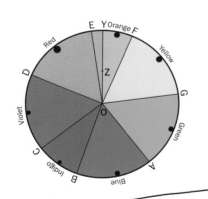

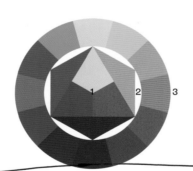

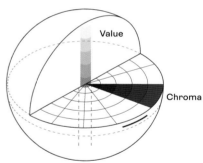

Newton's Color Circle
Issac Newton, in 1671, was the first to understand that colors did not lay on a linear trajectory, but rather existed in a continuous sequence. The resultant disk is represented by white at the center (O) and the hues arranged in order around the perimeter. Each hue is given a proportion that balances it within the system. Newton closed his system through a mix between red and violet that did not appear in his natural primary spectrum.

Itten's Color Wheel
In the 1930s, Johannes Itten began an exploration of color. A teacher at the Bauhaus, he developed a color wheel based on the primary colors (red, green, and blue). From this simple starting point(1), a secondary step(2) results in a 12-hue color circle(3). From this foundation, he developed a system of understanding complementary colors using seven rules of contrast.

Munsell's Color Sphere
Simultaneous with Itten, Albert Munsell, an American painter and teacher, developed a dimensional color system. In this system, hue is arranged around the perimeter of a sphere, value changes from light to dark as it moves from the top pole (light) to the bottom (dark); and chroma changes as it moves toward the center. Munsell also developed nomenclature that made it easy to identify any color in his system. For example, R 5/10 would be red, value 5, chroma 10.

In the SolBe Learning Center, the firm Supernormal uses colorful objects to break down the classroom into "dwelling" and "yard" zones.

A Note on Color Blindness

Those with the genetic condition of color blindness do not perceive colors the same way that the majority of the population does. Designers should know how this affects the use of color in the selection of palettes.

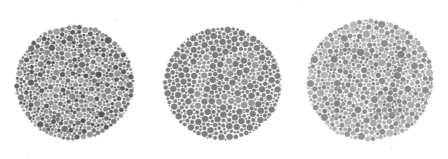

Ishihara color test plates, which test for red-green color deficiencies.

20 Composition

A visual arrangement in which separate elements come together to form a whole.

See Also
Emphasis
Layering
Proportion
Unity

Composition in interior design is the subtle art of arranging elements so that the overall spatial effect is related to a larger sequence of movement and repose.

As with proportion, ideas about composition are hard to quantify, and are often subjective ideas that can relate to a number of cultural and formal ideas. Some designers may aim for minimalist framing, while others develop more aggregated forms of composition. In addition, elements used in compositions can be established by location and theme—a Thonet chair can act as a compositional guide in a café setting, but look out of place in a large lobby space.

Composition is also not a singular thing. Arranging elements in an interior is a difficult and complex skill to hone. Whimsical placement of objects may elicit a joyous reaction, while a rigidly formal composition suggests quiet reflection. Each project will have its own compositional needs, and the configuration of elements is a way to begin to use design as an emotive tool.

The aptly named *Composition* (1916) by Dutch painter, Piet Mondrian is comprised of simple geometric elements and repeated use of primary colors and black.

A large Nanimarquina rug designed by Jaime Haylon anchors this coworking lounge in WeWork in Paris, France, while artwork and bright furnishings are arranged around it.

A calming palette of deep charcoal and warm white contrast harmoniously with wood wall paneling and a brass lighting fixture to carefully compose an elevation in a guest bedroom.

21 Connection

A logical relation, sequence, or association.

See Also
Biophilia
Character
Red Thread
Styling

The word *connection* has many connotations in interior design. It can refer to sequence, or the act of moving from exterior to interior, and the transitional spaces of lobbies, foyers, elevators and stairs that facilitate movement through a building or interior.

Connection also applies to the physical and visual relationships between spaces and rooms. This can be achieved by incorporating design elements like color and texture, such as using a consistent base color as the start of a palette. Similarly, the consistent use of finishes and styles can foster associations between rooms or pieces of furniture, which can contribute to a sense of coherence in a project. Physical elements in a space, an open stair, an aperture, and other openings, or the use of double-height volumes to connect between floors, provide literal transitions between rooms and functions.

More abstractly, connection can be considered the link between old (the existing condition) and new (the designed intervention). Through coordination with the architecture of the project, and careful integration of new partitions, furnishings, and built-in elements, and material selection and styling, the designer can bridge eras and typologies.

Another important connection in interior design is its relationship with nature. Through the incorporation of plants, the selection of natural materials, and the strategic use of water features and natural light, the designer can provide a connection to nature, and occasionally to outdoor spaces themselves.

Finally, interior design can foster an emotional or sensory connection, which elicits an association to a memory. This can be achieved through the design of lighting, the development of a color story that affects the general mood of a space, or through the integrations of elements during styling—photographs, mementos, art, or keepsakes.

The vertical expression of the wood paneling, combined with the striated pattern of the board-formed concrete link materials spatially in this São Paulo apartment by BC Arquitetos.

Glass partitions and a thin steel stair give visual access and indicate vertical connection in this Boston residence by OverUnder.

A living wall and waterfall in the Museum of Science in Boston links an atrium space with a view of the Charles River.

22 Contrast

The placement of two or more different design elements side by side to create an interesting effect.

See Also
Character
Color Theory
Scale
Shape

Helpful Advice
Contrast is most effective when applied strongly, when it draws the eye to a focal point in the design; ineffective use of contrast may cause confusion.

Contrast is a foundational and fundamental design principle. Also referred to as *juxtaposition*, contrast ensures that the elements of a room draw the eye while still maintaining a cohesive vision. It is important to know where and how to use contrast in an interior project. Contrast can make a room memorable or more impactful, add visual interest, and simultaneously pull together parts of a space. Contrasting elements (several are outlined below) add character to a design. Placing contrasting objects together can emphasize their differences.

Color is often the easiest way to add contrast to a room or space. The juxtaposition can be in the form of a color's brightness, temperature, intensity, or hue. Other methods include using different design styles, mixing furniture from different historical periods (i.e., placing an antique dresser in a contemporary hotel room), or applying varied textures. As a rule, a designer should consider binary opposites (of a surface or element, smooth and rough textures, rounded with geometric shapes or in scale) as a starting point for exploring juxtaposition of elements.

Various furniture elements, artwork, and lighting combine to give visual and textural contrast to a living room.

Color	Brightness	Light/Dark
	Temperature	Warm/Cool
	Hue	Red/Green
		Yellow/Purple
		Blue/Orange
	Intensity	Saturated/Desaturated

Shape		Organic/Geometric
	Edges	Sharp/Rounded
		Straight/Curved

Texture		Rough/Smooth
		Glossy/Matte
		Hard/Soft

Scale		Small/Large

Style		Antique/Modern
		Solid Color/Patterned
		Natural/Artificial

The Sunnyside Townhouse by AAMP Studio in Toronto, Ontario, celebrates contrast with a classic black and white color combination. Additionally, the rounded elements surrounding the fireplace and kitchen cabinet knobs contrast nicely with the rectilinear edges of the built-in cabinets and angles of the custom stair.

23 Craft

The expression of the fabrication of an interior or a design element that references quality and form.

See Also
Detail
Furniture
Innovation
Materiality

Craft is an important part of a successful interior. A well-crafted interior demonstrates the passion, attention to detail, and skills of fabricators, and highlights the connections that are an integral part of the making of an object—be it a wooden arm on a chair, a smooth plaster finish, or a finely articulated surface. Becoming proficient at working with a particular material or technique is a lifelong pursuit, and often incorporates the history of a technique. The current renaissance of designer-makers using elemental materials and working by hand, some referencing styles and techniques used centuries ago, points to design's continued investment in skilled artisanal production.

Ottoman Empire
Influenced by Byzantium, the Arab culture of the Islamic Middle East, and the Persian culture of Iran. Known for rich patterning and motifs (often religious) across designs for carpet weaving, textile arts, and metalsmithing (jewelry and cutlery).

Arts and Crafts Movement
Belief in craftpersonship, the inherent beauty of material, nature as inspiration, and the values of simplicity, unity, and beauty.

Bauhaus
Founded by Walter Gropius in 1919 in Weimar, Germany, and described as a "utopian craft guild combining architecture, sculpture, and painting into a single creative expression" and a craft-based curriculum for artists and designers to make beautiful objects.

Shaker
A style whose guiding principles are utility, simplicity, honesty, and minimalism. Made by the Shakers, a self-sufficient religious community, utilizing locally sourced wood as their main material. Functional in form and proportion.

Mingei
A Japanese movement established by Yanagi Sōetsu in the 1920s, framed around the philosophic pillar of "ordinary craft" and the beauty of functional, utilitarian, and everyday objects. It arose around the time of increasing industrialization and urban growth.

Types of Craft

Woodworking
Cabinets, Furniture

Textiles
Weaving, Blankets,
Pillows, Wall Hangings,
Rugs

Metalworking
Lighting, Cutlery

Ceramics
Tableware

Plaster
Walls, Surfaces,
Decorative Elements

Designed by Studio Gorm,
the 10 Degree Table for
Corral is made from solid
white oak.

Nao Tamura's Quill
rug, designed for
Nanimarquina, is hand
tufted from 100% wool.

Danish

Developed mid-century
(1950s), featuring func-
tionalist furniture and architecture. Architect and
furniture designer Kaare
Klint was known as the
father of modern Danish
furniture and established
a program through the
Royal Danish Academy of
Fine Arts.

24 Creativity

The discovery and imagining of new ideas.

See Also
Design Process
Discovery
Innovation
Inspiration

Although creativity is rooted in innovation, interiors often draw inspiration from what came before, what are prevailing ideas about style and taste, and what new solutions can be implemented to make a project more compelling and successful. As a designer, being creative is often more than making an aesthetic decision. Innovations can come in surprising forms—a new use for materials, a surprising placement of an object in space, or new technologies to deliver a project.

The creative designer looks for opportunities within a project or brief to develop solutions that attract curiosity and establish a leading voice in the profession. In return, this can enable competitive advantages to obtaining work, which often leads to clients who are open to new and adventurous ideas.

Conceptually, creativity is bolstered by research, curiosity, and an openness to separating from the habitual responses we have to a design problem. It can be facilitated by a consistent effort to be enlightened by and engage with continued education, and by teaching and attending student reviews. It also comes in forms and images found when exploring all manner of environments—shadows on a wall or patterns of objects in an urban environment.

Stacked cornice moldings form walls and counters in this Aesop store in Boston, Massachusetts, designed by WOJR.

The artist's studio in the atelier of the Italian artist and decorator Francesca Zoboli.

The facade of affordable workspace Yardhouse in Stratford, London, is designed by Assemble and consists of layered shingles in pastel tones.

25 Depth

The distance from top to bottom or front to back.

See Also
Aperture
Detail
Proportion
Surface

Usable space is at a premium in most projects, and depth, both real and implied, has the ability to make small spaces seem larger, make entrances more emphatic, or create opportunities for seating and rest in places carved into windows, walls, floors, or ceilings.

Depth can also be emphasized through the layering of elements, or by using dark colors or reflective surfaces. Painting a wall a deep shade can visually push that element further away from the viewer. Reflective surfaces, mirrors, or translucent surfaces can add implied space to a wall surface—especially when luminous materials are used, or backlighting creates the illusion of space.

Niches, alcoves, thresholds, open cabinets, and shelving are all ways to enhance spatial depth, and changes in elevation—either in a floor or ceiling plane—can add unexpected heights to a volume. Revealing depth in a surface is also an opportunity for cove lighting, wall wash illumination, and ambient light solutions.

The depth of walkways to hold bookshelves and books, the uplit arches of the ceiling and accentuate volume, the open circulation and natural light gives a sense of layer and depth to this room at the Rijksmuseum in Amsterdam.

Oslo studio Sanden+Hodnekvam Arkitekter's use of open shelving and windows adds spatial depth to rooms in this housing project in Lillehammer.

26 Design Process

The sequence (or order) of a project from conception to conclusion.

See Also
Collaboration
Discovery
Prototyping
Specifications

The process of a design project is defined by a meticulous progression from the generic to the specific. Arriving at a final design is an iterative process that incorporates all of the pieces of the concept into a cohesive whole.

The design process typically includes these phases predesign and programming, conceptual design, design development, pricing, and documentation and observation. For some projects, conceptual design and design development are combined; for others, a post-occupancy evaluation (or POE) is performed after the users have occupied the space to measure the success of the project.

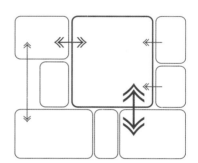

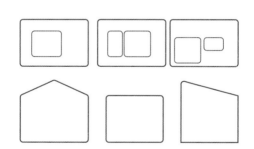

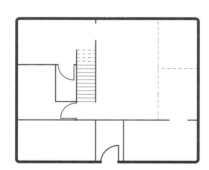

Predesign/Programming
This phase is the moment of identification, analysis, and documentation of the client's needs and goals, typically as a list that enumerates size of spaces, adjacencies, and sequence. This document then becomes the basis for evaluating any resultant design solution.

Conceptual Design
This is the most dynamic phase of the design process, where multiple options are considered and evaluated against programming. Mood boards, precedent imagery, and initial plan and volumetric tests are used to gain client consensus for a single design direction.

Design Development
Once major decisions have been made, the most design-intensive phase of the project begins. All design elements are developed, including all room and open space layouts; wall, window, floor, and ceiling treatments; furnishings, fixtures, and millwork; color, finishes, and hardware; and lighting, electrical, and communication systems.

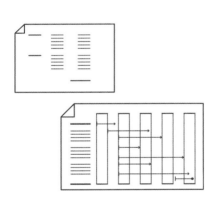

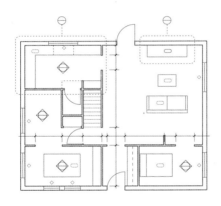

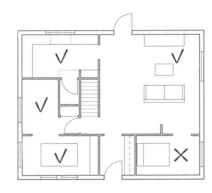

Pricing

At this point, a pricing exercise should be done with a consultant to determine that the project is achievable on the client's budget.

Documentation

Prior to starting construction, working drawings, details, and specifications are prepared to establish the methods of fabrication for non–load-bearing interior construction, materials, finishes, furnishings, fixtures, and equipment.

Observation

Administration of contract documents. Acting as the client's representative, the designer must approve shop drawings (which are translations of design elements such as built-in cabinets and sample confirmation), and visit the site frequently during construction to ensure that the project is being built according to the documents.

27 Detail

The documentation that describes the connection of materials.

See Also
Craft
Finishes
Materiality
Surface

The application of details in interior design refers to the design of the many smaller elements in a project. For some designers, it is the connections between materials, for others, it is the addition of elements like pattern and textiles that enhance a design. Details are the ways in which an interior comes together in a cohesive way.

Designers are tasked with communicating the design of details to fabricators and contractors, indicating how materials join, and explaining the tolerances—the level of precision in measurement—that are expected on the project. These subtle decisions are not immediately noticeable to a user or occupant, but if implemented well, they will be revealed over time. Attention to details also allows designers to use objects in unexpected ways, such as designing a custom shape on a plaster wall, or innovatively using materials to elevate a design.

To have a final design come together comprehensively, a lot of time, care, and effort needs to be given to coordinating the development of the space, from drawings through to the built form.

An articulated wall, artwork, lighting, and furniture bring detail to a light-filled dining room.

These are some of the elements in a design that require the use of details

Technical
Elements that make the fabrication of a design possible. Wall types and assemblies, millwork and joinery methods, standard heights and dimensions of objects, openings and material use (built-up floors), lighting integration, doors and transitions between material.

Aesthetic
Elements that enhance the visual and tactile appeal of a space. Tile and floor patterns, upholstery types, window coverings, surface types, opacity of materials, reflective elements, feature lighting elements.

Accessories
Items that are not integral to a solution. Choices of furniture, artwork, books, and other objects that fall into the realm of decoration; certain types of lighting to emphasize the details of a space.

Universal Principles of Interior Design

Sublime details
and coordination of
contractors can elevate
a project to new levels.
The subtlety of this is
evident in Splyce Design's
Highridge House in
Vernon, British Columbia.

A pulled-plaster wall
frames a doorway in
a loft in Tribeca, New
York, designed by
Young Projects.

28 Discovery

The initial phase of a design process between the client and designer.

See Also
Collaboration
Design Process
Modeling
Prototyping

Discovery refers to the initial phase of a design project, during which the interior designer seeks to uncover the needs, connections, attitudes, and opinions that a client or group might have toward a project. The discovery phase collects, organizes, and synthesizes the data needed to begin developing space planning and sketch plans, and uses various methods to elicit knowledge and needs from various users. These can take the form of programming, meetings, and focus group sessions with stakeholders, sketching exercises that help determine scope and adjacency; and the establishment of benchmarks that point to a successful end result or product. This is a very important phase, involving both the client and design team, and the process necessitates in-depth discussions and meetings to help shape goals and visual concepts for the project.

In addition, the evaluation of the existing conditions of a project is critical during this phase. Through assessment, evaluation, and the collection and scrutiny of existing documentation through site surveying, the discovery phase evaluates the feasibility of a space or building to contain the program being developed. In certain cases, it is advisable to engage with a contractor, construction management company, or owner's project manager. These consultants act as a liaison between designer and client, and help ensure that budget and schedule are considered at the beginning of a project.

The outcome of a discovery process should provide the foundation on which the next phase of development occurs, and establishes baselines to which the goals of the project can be measured. In some cases, a report or guide is delivered to the client team as a document.

Universal Principles of Interior Design

The design by Hacin + Associates for IDEO's offices in a former parking garage in Cambridge, Massachusetts, includes several types of workspaces to foster programmatic flexibility.

Examining the needs of a project involves looking closely at the needs of a client, space allocations, and adjacencies.

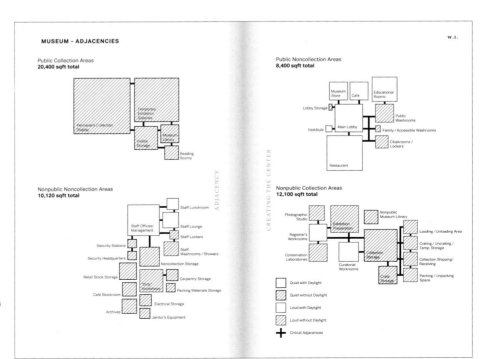

W.I.

MUSEUM - ADJACENCIES

Public Collection Areas
20,400 sqft total

Permanent Collection Display
Temporary Exhibition Galleries
Visible Storage
Museum Library
Reading Rooms

Public Noncollection Areas
8,400 sqft total

Museum Store
Café
Educational Rooms
Lobby Storage
Public Washrooms
Vestibule
Main Lobby
Family / Accessible Washrooms
Cloakrooms / Lockers
Restaurant

Nonpublic Noncollection Areas
10,120 sqft total

Staff Lunchroom
Staff Offices/ Management
Staff Lounge
Staff Lockers
Security Stations
Staff Washrooms / Showers
Security Headquarters
Noncollection Storage
Retail Stock Storage
Carpentry Storage
Café Stockroom
Dirty Workshops
Packing Materials Storage
Electrical Storage
Archives
Janitor's Equipment

Nonpublic Collection Areas
12,100 sqft total

Photographic Studio
Exhibition Preparation
Nonpublic Museum Library
Registrar's Workrooms
Loading / Unloading Area
Conservation Laboratories
Collection Storage
Crating / Uncrating / Temp. Storage
Curatorial Workrooms
Collection Shipping/ Receiving
Crate Storage
Packing / Unpacking Space

Quiet with Daylight
Quiet without Daylight
Loud with Daylight
Loud without Daylight
+ Critical Adjacencies

ADJACENCY

CREATING THE CENTER

29 Durability

The quality of being designed to exist for a long time without significant deterioration in condition or value.

See Also
Finish
Furniture
Materiality
Specifications

The durability of an object is typically measured in use, life span, and operation, but it is also important to consider the level of maintenance of objects and the environmental impacts that affect decisions surrounding utility and expense. Materials selection is critical to the quality of a finished project, and should be selected according to how well they withstand daily use.

More recently, the expression "emotionally durable design" describes an approach to sustainable design that aims to reduce the consumption and waste of natural resources through increasing the reliability and functionality in the products users choose. Based on behavior and use, products that create emotional connections, and produce durable solutions in the design of lasting products that are less expendable, will be cherished for longer periods.

An interior designer's selection of materials, furniture, and finishes can impact the environment and have a positive effect on the users of a space. Through research, testing, and selection, the durability of a material improves appearance, comfort, and the long-term success of a project.

Hospitals and healthcare facilities hold high standards and requirements for hygienic and durable materials. Steelcase combines technology and mobility with cleanable and sturdy surfaces to develop furniture specifically for healthcare.

Flooring

The surface that receives the most impact and wear in an interior is the floor. Use and type should be considered as factors for selection, as well as the need to be refinished, be resistant to scratches and stains, and be the appropriate resiliency for use. Types of flooring include rubber, vinyl, porcelain tile, linoleum, terrazzo, and carpet (broadloom or tile).

Upholstery

The life span of furniture can be improved when extremely durable and high performance textiles are specified. All textiles must pass highly rigorous testing that evaluates a material based on cleanability, stretching, and fraying by review of "double rubs" and how color fast it is when adjacent to natural light sources.

Wall Surfaces

Wall surfaces in high traffic areas need to be adequately protected from the objects that bang into or rub against them or leave permanent marks. Solid materials, such as stone and high-density wood, require little maintenance. For gypsum walls, refinishing is critical to durability. Some low-cost options are low-VOC paints, and vinyl and textile wall coverings. High performance coatings, designed for protection and performance, provide antimicrobial protection.

Hard Surfaces

Materials used for millwork, counters, built-in shelving, and other elements. Natural stone, ceramics, plastic laminates, and solid surface materials are easily maintained and withstand heavy use over time. When specifying hard surfaces, it is important to confirm impact testing, and the suitability of the material for horizontal or vertical applications.

30 Egress

The place or means of going out; exit.

See Also
Accessibility
Circulation
Codes
Occupancy

Helpful Advice
Clearly marked exit signs must follow local building regulations prior to building occupancy.

Codes and standards that regulate a building's means of egress system will vary depending on the use of the particular building, area, or room, and can be complicated. Egress means exit and is an important part of all building codes for the safety of the occupants.

Some of these requirements include (but are not limited to) the following determining maximum occupant load depending on the number of exits; determining direction of door swings (typically out) based on maximum occupant load; doors that require panic hardware; the location and required number of automatic sprinklers; the requirement that exit doors have direct adjacency to exit corridors or stairwells (and not to pass through adjacent spaces); calculating size of exit doors based on occupant load; the placement of exit and entry signs; and the installation of luminous path markings.

Some of these calculations fall outside the role of an interior designer, so code consultants should be engaged. Nevertheless, the designer should be aware of and involved in the necessary precautions and the impact of the design of the space.

This way to the Egress

Famous showman P.T. Barnum's popular American Museum would often be too crowded, so P.T. installed signs that read "This way to the Egress" as if it were another attraction similar to "To the Clown Show," leading people out the exit door, which locked behind them and forced them to pay for another ticket to regain entry.

In some cases (such as an auditorium where people exit through a lobby), egress through an adjacent room (the lobby) is acceptable. For rooms with fixed seating (such as auditoriums), occupant load should not exceed the number of fixed seats, plus the number of designated wheelchair spaces, if provided. The occupant load for the stage or platform should be calculated separately from the seating area.

31 Emphasis

The center of interest or focal point of a composition.

See Also
Alignment
Composition
Harmony
Placement

When speaking, emphasizing something means calling attention to a particular word or phrase. Similarly, in interior design, emphasis is used to direct attention to a specific design element—a freestanding object, a wall element, or a lighting fixture—within a volume. Emphasis can be used to allow for visual pause, to direct an occupant through a sequence of spaces, or to reduce or punctuate the acoustics of a room sonically.

Emphasis is an important tactic in interior design. By highlighting the room's focal point, the designer can direct the viewer's attention to a specific location. A space without a focal point can come across as scattered rather than cohesive or harmonious.

There are two methods of emphasis that a designer can deploy

Emphasis by Strategic Placement.
This method varies by project type. In a retail interior, clients may request to emphasize signage, products or customer service counters. A commercial office might emphasize elements in a lobby, or lead users toward meeting or event spaces. In a home, artwork, a large window or dramatic double height spaces function as the focal points.

Emphasis by Design Elements.
By deploying items that contrast color, pinpoint light, highlight form, texture, or patterns, the designer is able to draw the eye toward elements. An amazing view through a large opening, gallery, or mosaic-tiled wall is an example of emphasis by multiple elements. Acoustically, an intimate space lined with soft material can isolate sound and suggest comfort and rest.

There are several different ways to add emphasis

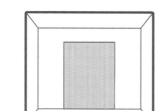

Emphatic
Natural or architectural focal point. Prominent and clearly featured.

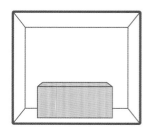

Dominant
Any feature added to completely dominate the design of a space.

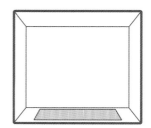

Subdominant
Smaller features such as rugs, curtains, and central furniture.

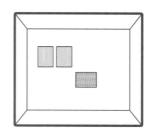

Subordinate
Includes accessories and small featured décor.

In the Teca House in Biella, Italy, designed by Federico Delrosso, the strategic placement of low furniture allows the large windows and the views of the surrounding hillside landscape to become the focal point.

Kuchar hung a chandelier grouping of thirty IKEA pendants at the headquarters of Farmer's Fridge, a Chicago, Illinois start-up that brings fresh salads to vending machines around the city.

32 Ergonomics

The study of the ways in which the human body occupies space.

See Also
Adaptability
Health, Safety,
and Welfare
Human Scale
Universal Design

Further Reading
*Ergonomics in Design
The Quarterly of Human
Factors Applications,*
journals.sagepub.com/
home/erg

Derived from the Greek words *ergon* (meaning work) and *noms* (meaning laws), ergonomic design is the practice of utilizing and designing spaces and furniture that remove incompatibilities between the work being done and the human body.

The main focus area of research in ergonomics is the workplace. Due to the nature of office work, it is important to tune the workplace to suit the needs of employees, who spend approximately one-third of their time there. Preventing injury or musculoskeletal disorders (MSDs) and repetitive stress injuries (RSIs) is critical for long-term health and wellness. Ergonomics provides the tools necessary to prevent undue strain on the body and reduce physical discomfort due to repetitive tasks and movements.

At its foundation, ergonomics has evolved from the study of anthropometry, which refers to measurement of the physical properties of the human body—specifically body size and shape. It acknowledges that not every human body is alike, and that our collective capabilities and limitations vary.

The benefits of incorporating ergonomics into the workplace include higher productivity among employees, better product quality, increased employee engagement, enhanced mental health and wellness, and an improved culture of safety.

Office Seating
Reduce physical discomfort,
increases flexibility.

Ergonomic Products / Functions and Benefits

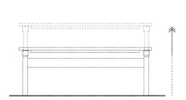

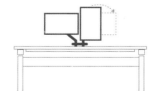

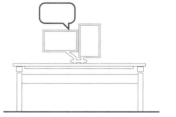

Adjustable-Height Tables
Support flexible work styles; standing places less stress on the spine.

Technology Accessories
Monitor arms offer a flexible work setup, prevent eye strain, and reduce risk of injury

Behavioral Technology
Software that encourages movement, visual breaks, walks, and more frequent changes in postures.

Casual Furniture
Accommodates a variety of postures, flexibility; supports changing technology.

33 Finishes

The level of detail on the final surfaces or surface types of a design project.

See Also
Craft
Detail
Materiality
Surface

Reference
*Mohsen Mostafavi, David Leatherbarrow, *On Weathering The Life of Buildings in Time* (MIT Press, 1993).

Finishes are everywhere in an interior—whether it is the touch of a door upon entering a room, the softness of a carpet underfoot, or the glare of a mirror in the daylight. We experience and determine the appropriate finishes for a design through our senses of touch, vision, hearing, and smell, and each layers upon the last to create our experience of a space.

Finishes are also temporal, in that they are affected by wear and tear, and use over time—metallic elements gain patina, railings register the oils of a hand's touch, leather softens. The British post–World War II architects Alison and Peter Smithson referred to this as "the art of inhabitation," in which finishes and occupants age simultaneously. Or, as the critics Mohsen Mostafavi and David Leatherbarrow say in their book *On Weathering The Life of Buildings in Time**, "finishing ends construction, weather constructs finishes."

For interiors, weather is less of a factor in the maturation of finish, but through use, wear, and the microclimates of spaces that change with heat and moisture, finishes adapt and change. In essence, the aging of interior finishes gives character to a space. At a certain point, the effects of aging on finishes indicate when a space needs an intervention in the form of renovation and renewal.

The subtle contrast of an existing column against sympathetic finishes develops a narrative about the durability and patina of finish in this Soho loft by BC—OA.

A number of finishes in Bestor Architecture's headquarters for Beats are complemented by a Tasili rug by Sandra Figuerola for Gan Rugs.

The natural aging and patina of a wood wall can add character and texture to a space.

34 Form

The recognizable shape of an object or a space.

See Also
Geometry
Organic
Shape
Volume

Form is the perception and shape of a room as well as any objects or elements in that room, including furniture, lighting, or built-in features. Anything that has three dimensions of height, width, and depth is considered form.

In an interior, there are two main classifications of form

Geometric These are objects whose form does not occur in nature. They are synthetic forms whose shape is described by hard lines and edges. Some geometric objects also are made of curvilinear elements and rounded forms. These shapes can appear softer and more relaxing. Often referred to as "Platonic solids," these shapes include cubes, cylinders, and spheres.

Natural These shapes either naturally occur in organic matter, such as flowers and plants, or are inspired by patterns or shapes derived from or influenced by nature.

Designers must recognize the proportions and scale of a space and consider the forms being placed within it. The addition of forms of a similar shape or size can increase harmony and balance. Conversely, adding too many differing forms can cause visual confusion or dissonance. Interiors are typically more pleasing when a dominant form is repeated in various objects throughout the space.

Frank Lloyd Wright's design for the Solomon R. Guggenheim Museum in New York City (1959) borrows its cylindrical shape—wider at the top than the bottom—from organic forms and functionally offers a unique experience within the spiral ramp gallery.

The curvilinear forms of
the Fog x FLO exhibition
by BOS|UA were
inserted into the strict
geometry of Boston's
Emerald Necklace
Conservancy's offices.

35 Function

The intended use of a space or environment.

See Also
Adaptability
Adjacency
Hybridization
Program

"Form follows function" has become a mantra since it was coined by the Chicago architect Louis Sullivan in his 1896 essay "The Tall Office Building Artistically Considered." In practice, the phrase dictates that the use of a space should be the determining factor in the development of a design. Sullivan's investment in maximizing the design of an emerging typology—the skyscraper—relies on efficiency and consistency of program to determine the form, or shape, of his structures.

The role of function in interior design is often mistakenly perceived as at odds with the limited aesthetic scope that is traditionally associated with the profession. Increasingly, a functional approach to design solutions is at the essence of a process that "right sizes" rooms and gathering spaces, makes adjacencies efficient, and minimizes excessive circulation and wasted space. Extraneous decoration and ornamentation are set aside in favor of use and type.

In smaller urban spaces, multiple uses often occur in the same space, which can lead to inventive and compelling solutions that allow for the use of a space to change over time.

The repeating elements of recognizable retail environments indicate the function of the Hyundai Mall in Seoul, South Korea, by Richard Rogers.

The shape of an auditorium is determined by the performances or lectures that take place inside it.

A small workshop and retail space in Somerville, Massachusetts, by Loyal Union features multifunctional walls and movable elements to maximize the use.

36 Furniture

The movable elements in a design that provide functional support.

See Also
Adaptability
Finishes
Function
Modularity

Knowledge of the history of furniture and exemplary examples of furnishings is foundational in an interior designer's toolkit. The most pedantic definition of a piece of furniture is that it is something that supports human activities that take place in an interior.

Although seating, tables, beds, cabinetry, and other items for storage can be considered from a purely functional perspective, furniture also has an aesthetic and decorative function is what makes the choice of elements one of the most consequential decisions in a project. Items can be chosen to fulfill an appropriate need in a project, or to be used as a signature element that is meant to elicit a sense of delight that would make a user pause and take notice.

From the earliest examples from Egypt, Greece, and Rome, or the traditions of Indian, Chinese, or Japanese craft, furniture has also served to symbolize position and importance. In particular, the chair has symbolized authority (e.g., the seat of power, sit at the head of the table). Other decorative and applied elements are used as narrative devices to signify the importance of history and position.

In the twentieth century, furniture became a device for radical functionalism, material exploration, and whimsical and colorful forms. From the early experimentation of the Bauhaus, the postwar use of plywood by Charles and Ray Eames, the foundation of the commercial furniture market with companies like Steelcase and Herman Miller, the emergence of the Italian design and architecture group Memphis, and the development of flat-pack and IKEA, to the major fairs around the world dedicated to them, our need to express ourselves through furniture continues to evolve.

Universal Principles of Interior Design

A house with shelves from 3180–2500 CE. found in Scotland.

An Egyptian chair from 1492–1473 CE.

A Chinese canopy bed from the late nineteenth or early twentieth century.

Gerrit Rietveld's *Red and Blue Chair*, 1917.

Charles Eames, *Leg Splint*, designed 1941–1942.

Several other pieces by Hella Jongerius, including the custom designed East River Chair (2014) furnish the United Nations North Delegates' lounge.

37 Geometry

The measurement, properties, and relationships of points, lines, angles, surfaces, and solids to each other.

See Also
Form
Organic
Shape
Volume

The word *geometry* comes from the ancient Greek root words *geo* meaning earth and *metron*, meaning measurement, and is one of the oldest branches of mathematics. As applied to interior design, it is primarily concerned with the properties of space related to distance, shape, size, and position of objects or figures. Geometry also has similar connections with art, architecture, and graphic design.

In interiors, math and, in particular, geometry are important for several of the specialties a designer is expected to be knowledgeable about calculation of area to specify materials like flooring, drapery, and upholstery; understanding volume and three-dimensional properties, including height, width, and depth; the measurement and relationship of elements based on angles; the synchronization and establishment of patterns and themes within a space; space planning and room layout; and the placement of furniture and decor based on the size and shape of each element.

A platonic solid is a regular, convex polyhedron, constructed by congruent (same shape and size), regular (all angles equal and all sides equal) with same number of faces meeting at each vertex. The five platonic solids are cube, dodecahedron, tetrahedron, octahedron, and icosahedron.

Cube   Tetrahedron   Octahedron   Dodecahedron   Icosahedron

Universal Principles of Interior Design

Sacred geometry is based on symbolic and sacred attributes given to specific geometric shapes and proportions with the belief that a deity is the geometer of the world. Sacred geometry is often used in the design of religious spaces like churches, temples, and mosques, as seen in early Moroccan architecture.

The Keep Vessel, by Kelly Harris Smith for Corral, uses a geometric twist to develop its form.

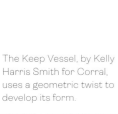

The architecture of the Saadian Tombs in Morocco are a testament to complex geometric form.

38 Gradation

The technique that uses a gradual shift in scale, texture, or color to generate visual movement or create perspective.

See Also
Color Theory
Finishes
Monochrome
Surface

Like rhythm in interior design, gradation can create visual movement with a progression of elements that shift gradually. Gradation stems from the Latin word *gradus*, meaning "step" and "degree."

The three prominent uses of gradation in interior design are scale, color and texture

Leonardo da Vinci's *Study of the Graduations of Shadows on Spheres* (1492).

Three Houses by Paul Klee (1922), watercolor on paper, uses gradated tones of blues, greens, and violets.

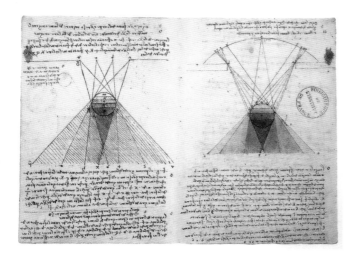

Scale
Perhaps the simplest way to understand gradation is to line up objects from small to large. The shift in size can instantly move the eye across the objects. Gradated scale can be found in size and placement of furniture, patterned textiles, or even in light fixtures. Strategically spacing objects (e.g., lighting or decor) can also generate the appearance of gradated scale and movement.

Color
Gradated color can involve a single hue, successively shifting opacity, or shade, tint, or multiple colors gradating from one color to another. For example, gradation in color from red to blue would also include tones of purple where the two colors overlap.

Texture
Gradation in texture is more difficult to perceive, but can be achieved by changing finishes from matte to glossy or shifting textures from smooth to rough.

Dutch firm i29 celebrates color and whimsy in their restoration of Felix Meritis, a historic civic building in Amsterdam. Each space is designed to reference colors and materials from a particular time period.

39 Grid

A framework of lines at right angles to each other.

See Also
Alignment
Composition
Emphasis
Hierarchy

Grids are important organizing elements that enable designers to measure, place, and organize objects on surfaces and in a space. Grids also have an impact on scale; small aggregated elements arranged in a grid can make spaces feel more graphic, and bring both a visual and tactile motif to a design strategy.

Wall coverings that are used in an interior are by the nature of their design often aggregated into grids, and many types of floor coverings also come in different, incremental dimensions that make them useful in laying out spaces and elements.

Volumetric grids have physical depth. Many structural systems used in a building provide opportunity for grids as organizing devices for a space. A waffle slab—a concrete construction system—can inform how walls are placed, and how elements are arranged underneath. Deep-cell ceiling treatments can also be used for a similar effect.

Open shelves and thinner elements and details can also impact how a wall surface is perceived, and panelized walls offer yet another grid-based system for coordination.

For his 2013 Serpentine Gallery Pavilion, Sou Fujimoto designed a delicate three-dimensional array of painted white poles that suggests enclosure.

Bookshelves are good examples of organizing grids. This collection by Montana Furniture in Denmark uses unexpected divisions to enhance the grid.

The Rafael Santa Ana Architecture Workshop designed a double-height shelving system to unify two floors of a house in Vancouver, British Columbia.

40 Harmony

The aesthetically pleasing agreement of parts in a composition.

See Also

Balance
Depth
Emphasis
Form
Proportion

In musical theory, harmony is the composition of sounds, consisting of simultaneous pitches, rhythms, or chords, and the process of analysis and interpretation by listening or hearing those sounds. Similarly, in interior design, harmony is the way all of the elements in a space combine in a manner to create a pleasing experience for the occupants and users. Designers use harmony to help the senses comprehend the totality of a space, and to understand it as an aggregation of various elements that promote a calming and relaxing interior.

Color harmony can be implemented through the use of a single tone, or can vary in hue or value to unite a space together with the furnishings and objects it contains. Sound can also be used, whether ambient by the active sounds in a space, or through dampening and clamping of reverberation via textiles and acoustic baffles. Touch is also in play, but in a much more subtle way. Using mainly soft surfaces and eliminating hard edges from a design eases movement through a space.

In addition to these, other design elements like furniture or accessories can work together to harmonize based on shape, size, placement, texture, and rhythm.

A note of caution The reliance on a single, repetitive element in a composition can be detrimental to an interior concept. Careful consideration of placement, and subtle variations in surfaces can elevate the emotional resonance of a room, and keep harmony from becoming monotonous.

Feng Shui is the Chinese design philosophy that seeks to find balance and harmony among all elements. The terms *feng* for "wind" and *shui* for "water" are the two basic elements driving this reasoning with the goal of positioning different elements to optimize the *Chi*, or energy within a space. This is done with the incorporation of materials following the five natural elements of wood, metal, earth, water, and fire.

The placement of a central dining table, aligned with lighting above, and the symmetrical placement of a credenza and artwork work in harmony in this Boston residence designed by Jessica Klein.

Asymmetrical placement of RBW light fixtures, acoustic wall panels, and the soft curves of the banquet all work together to balance out this restaurant nook.

40 Harmony

41 Health, Safety, and Welfare

Implementing designs that prevent harm or injury caused by failure, breakage, or accident.

See Also
Accessibility
Circulation
Codes
Durability

Modern buildings are designed to be safe, healthy, and comfortable living and working environments. Both in design and maintenance, however, there is the potential for occupational illnesses and injuries, air quality and circulation issues, accidents, and exposure to hazardous materials. The designer, working with architects, engineers, and facility managers, aims to implement solutions and maintain spaces that ensure occupant safety and health. In a commercial space, this often takes the form of a manual for operation and maintenance of the building or space. In residential spaces, the user is primarily responsible for maintenance of the space or building.

The protection of health and safety has expanded to include mental and physical health, as well as protecting the ecological health of a place.

Health, Safety, and Welfare (HSW) concerns should be addressed in all phases of the design and life cycle of an interiors project, from planning through to construction. This includes maintenance, renovation and upkeep, and disposal of materials and waste. The designer should ensure compliance with the various municipal building codes, and environmental agencies and organizations that govern how these elements are transported and disposed of.

Interior designers can ensure the HSW of the occupants of a building or space by taking these actions

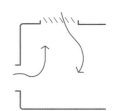

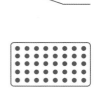

Eliminate or reduce hazards both physical and environmental.

Ensure good indoor air quality, ventilation, and rate of air exchange.

Provide safe and secure electrical service.

Prevent slips, trips, and falls, and occupational illnesses or injuries.

Design and Install ergonomic workspaces and furniture to prevent work-related injuries.

Routinely maintain and evaluate proper building operations.

Natural light, open space, contrasting materials, and wide stairs all contribute to the welfare of the employees at Bergmeyer's design for the office for Boston Dynamics.

Workplace designs that incorporate natural lighting, plants, and ergonomic and adaptable furniture contribute to the physical and mental health of employees.

42 Hierarchy

The arrangement of elements according to their value or to the relative importance they hold in a system.

See Also
Emphasis
Hierarchy
Placement
Proportion

Further Reading
Kenya Hara, *Haptic—Awakening the Senses* Exhibition. www.ndc.co.jp/hara/en/works/2014/08/haptic.html.com.

"Haptics and Vision in Architecture." Jasmien Herssens, Ann Heylighen, (2008).

Many disciplines define hierarchy as predominantly a visual term. In interior design, it can also be considered a spatial term, and, in a more complex way, haptic and aural phenomenons.

Treating hierarchy as a set of visual cues gives the designer authority over the narrative of a space. When we approach a room, either conceptually or literally, there is the total room—the openings and apertures that allow movement and light into the space, the objects that either invite movement or welcome stasis, specific colors or lights that act as indicators of tasks and use. Each element can become more visually dominant in order to suggest how a space can be used.

However, if we expand the visual-centric nature of hierarchy, we discover a richer range of possibilities. Haptic hierarchies are those that relate to the sense of touch. Different materials are used to elicit emotions or behaviors—for example, a tactile change in material on a floor or wall can indicate a change in use or can act as a cue for a necessary change in movement.

The sound of a room can also be emphasized. Within aural hierarchies, the value given to relative acoustics is a way to expand our sense of place. Echoey rooms can sound more active and energetic, while the introduction of acoustic baffles and surfaces can provide cues for mood and atmosphere.

The visual weight of this built-in nook, in contrast to the lighter adjacent materials, emphasizes use and function in this kitchen designed by Cecilia Casagrande Interiors.

In a children's bedroom by OverUnder, the bright colors of the felt wall also dampen sound and reverberation.

43 History

The study of the profession via its past.

See Also
Design Process
Discovery
Inspiration

Further Reading
Mitchell Owens, "The 25 Most Influential Interior Designers of the 20th Century," *Architectural Digest*, December 23, 2019, www.architecturaldigest.com/gallery/the-25-most-influential-interior-designers.

Grace Lees-Maffei, "Introduction Professionalization as a Focus in Interior Design History," *Journal of Design History*, www.nda.ac.uk/blog/interior-designer-or-architect/.

Any profession stands on the legacy of knowledge and prior discoveries, and while we are often eager to deny the influence of history on the contemporary design decisions that we make, the path to professionalization of interior design should be mentioned.

Interior design, as an occupation, has only existed for a short time, and the term *interior designer* has only been in use for less than a hundred years. The profession emerged out of the decorative arts and craft tradition, and has been shaped by developments in the industry that shifted it from one of decorating—the embellishment of a thing—to designing—the planner of form based on use and program.

In the latter half of the twentieth century, rapidly adopted standards and testing established a baseline of expertise. In 1957, the American National Society for Interior Designers was formed out of an earlier organization, the American Institute of Interior Decorators (1931). By the mid-twentieth century, several countries had established organizations such as the Finnish Association of Interior Architects (1949) and the Interior Decorators and Designers Association in the U.K. (1966). By the 1970s, multiple U.S. organizations merged to create the American Society of Interior Designers (ASID), which oversaw the accreditation of design programs formalized under the Foundation for Interior Design Education Research (FIDER). In 1974, the National Council for Interior Design Qualification Examination (NCIDQ) became the standard exam to test and promote guidelines for determining competency in the profession.

The relationship between the architecture and interior design professions remains contentious, where issues of responsibility, life safety, and liability are continuously debated, and professional agency is vigorously defended on both sides.

The American Society of Interior Designers and the Council for Interior Design Qualifications websites' home page.

The Salon de Verre (1932), designed by Paul Ruaud, was furnished with early pieces designed by Eileen Gray, a pioneer of modern furniture design.

The furniture collection at the Museum of Modern Art in New York.

44 Hue

The discernible attribute of a color.

See Also

Color Theory
Gradation
Monochrome
Tone

Color is a tool used by a designer to influence the external perception of an interior environment and internal psychology of the viewer. The concept of a system to organize color by hue was explored as early as 1810 with Philipp Otto Runge's *Color Sphere*. Later, the Munsell color system was developed by Albert H. Munsell in the 1930s.

The properties, or effects, of a color are determined by hue, value (light and dark), and chroma (purity). Hue is the dominant color seen. It can be viewed as the foundation of color. A hue is a pure color that is not mixed with white, gray, or black to create a tint, tone, or shade. Hues include primary, secondary, and tertiary colors.

Fitz Henry Lane's painting *Lumber Schooners at Evening on Penobscot Bay* (1863) captures the naturally occurring hues of a picturesque sunset over the Atlantic Ocean.

Blue hues, evoking the calm and serenity of the sky and the ocean, are found throughout this apartment in Barcelona, Spain, designed by The Room Studio.

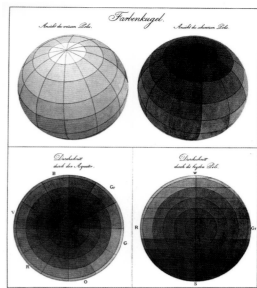

Color Sphere (Die Farben-Kugel) by German painter and draftsman Philippe Otto Runge (1810). Hues are labeled R, O, G, Gr, B, V for red, orange, yellow ("gelb" in German), green, blue, violet.

The top two diagrams show the surface of the sphere, while the bottom two show cross sections, vertical and horizontal.

45 Human-Centered Design

A process of discovery that forefronts human perspective.

See Also
Ergonomics
Health, Safety,
  and Welfare
Inclusivity
Universal Design

Reference
*Mike Cooley, *Architect
or Bee? The Human/
Technology Relationship*
(South End Press, 1982).

Further Reading
IDEO.org, *The Field
Guide to Human-
Centered Design*
(IDEO.org, 2015).
www.designkit.org

Human-centered design, first developed by Irish engineer Mike Cooley in 1989, began as an exploration of "human-centered systems, as used in economics, computing and design, that aim to preserve or enhance human skills, in both manual and office work, and in environments in which technology tends to undermine the skills that people use in their work."*

In interior design, it can be simply defined as the process of implementing a design solution through the inclusion and emphasis of human perspective at all phases of the design process.

The goals of human-centered design are to increase productivity, improve user experiences, reduce discomfort and stress, increase the usability of a space for people with a wide range of capabilities, and contribute to sustainability standards. This process leads to empathic design, which is an emotional and subjective approach to design solutions, rather than an overreliance on empirical data.

While the participatory focus of human-centered design is often lauded, it has also been criticized as an ineffective approach, that is too focused on present needs, that future and long-term design solutions are not taken into consideration. Others have criticized that the process may be dominated by one user or small group, or too broadly so that no specific group needs are fully addressed.

Architects and interior
designers work with
students, faculty,
administration, and
maintenance through
all stages of the design
process to effectively
come up with solutions
that work for all.

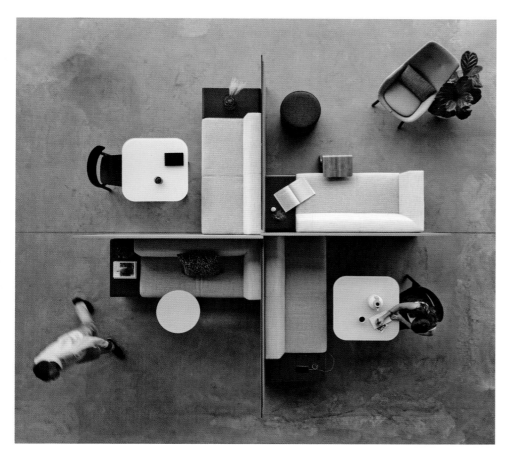

46 Human Scale

The physical qualities of the human body expressed in dimensions, capabilities, and limits.

See Also Ergonomics
Health, Safety, and Welfare
Inclusivity
Universal Design

How we interact with our environment is based on the physical and sensory capabilities of the human body. In the built environment, both new and renovated, interiors and functional elements such as the width of doorways, the minimum rise and run of stairways, the location of railings, the positioning of light switches, or the height of work surfaces are scaled to humans. Other sensory decisions include lines of sight through a space, the acoustic properties of a room, and adequate lighting for tasks.

Creating a human-scale interior environment involves making sure that elements are of a shape and size that is comfortable and reasonable for an average person to interact with. This is not without its own problematic issues, as insistence on the "ideal" or "average" ignores the reality of our able-centric world. Any discussion of human scale should include accommodations for different body types and levels of accessibility.

Leonardo Da Vinci's *Vitruvian Man* (1487) is based on the correlation of geometry and ideal human proportions as described by the ancient Roman architect Vitruvius.

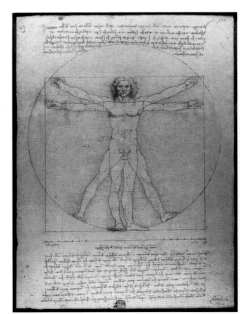

The Humanscale Manual by Henry Dreyfuss Associates, originally published between 1974 and 1981, is a quick reference guide for designing objects, interactions, and environments for humans with over sixty thousand measured diagrams.

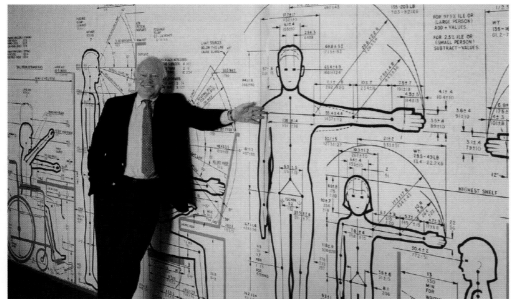

The kitchen is the most utilitarian room in a home. The placement of equipment and storage is based on human scale and interactions with the components of the room. This Parisian apartment by SABO project demonstrates this concept with a galley kitchen that integrates appliances and cabinetry in a minimal birch plywood.

47 Hybridization

The combination or integration of multiple styles, types, and functions.

See Also
Function
Furniture
Typology

Further Reading
Anne-Laure Fayard, John Weeks, and Mahwesh Khan, "Designing the Hybrid Office From Workplace to 'Culture Space'," *Harvard Business Review*, March–April 2021, hbr.org/2021/03/designing-the-hybrid-office.

Hybridization occurs when a space requires functional overlap, when an eclectic set of references or styles are implemented, or where a space may function as a social or cultural connector. There are several instances where products and spaces in interior design have a combination of functions or styles that enhance their usability.

As space becomes a premium, designing environments that serve more than one function is an incredibly useful skill for an interior designer to possess. The overlap and integration of fluid boundaries between the design of commercial, residential, retail, and healthcare spaces have made multifunctional and multi-use spaces and objects a rich field of investigation and discovery.

Hybridization as a design strategy speaks to function, promotes a sustainable attitude, and generally benefits the user by bolstering the ability of a design in performance, duration, and use. Spaces are now often required to be responsive to the changing needs of users.

It is also an integral approach to design and can be loosely gathered into the following categories

Purpose and Function
The design of multi-use furniture, for example a bench that is also a desk, or an environment that functions both as a lounge and collaborative workspace. Recent retail design practices blur the distinction between retail space and the workspace (a coffee shop and a bank) or a lounge and DJ booth in a clothing shop.

Style Mixing
Historical and regional influences, which celebrate the eclectic and the mixing of traditional design trends, such as Japandi —Japanese mixed with Scandinavian styles.

Product and Type
Products that are useful for a variety of purposes, the mix of old and new materials, or the combination of an old material with new technique of manufacturing.

Dirk van Der Kooij designed and built a machine to 3D print the Chubby Chair using an old factory robot to extrude hot plastic that comes from recycled refrigerators.

Many office interiors feel more like home, blurring the line between residential and commercial, lately nicknamed "resimercial." The "living room" and "dining room" are finished in comforting warm tones and materials associated with home but utilized in communal meeting or working spaces.

48 Inclusivity

Providing equal access and opportunity.

See Also
Accessibility
Design Process
Ergonomics
Universal Design

Further Reading
Design Council, "Inclusive Environments," www.designcouncil. org.uk/what-we-do/ built-environment/ inclusive-environments

Kat Holmes, *Mismatch How Inclusion Shapes Design* (MIT Press, 2018). katholmesdesign.com.

Stalled! www.stalled.online

The inclusive design of an environment is one that can be accessed and utilized by as many users as possible, especially those who have historically been excluded (because of race, gender, sexuality, class, or ability). This is a holistic practice, and is not simply relevant to buildings and their interior spaces, but also to surrounding open spaces, landscapes, and experiential design elements.

As defined by Susan Goltsman (FASLA 1949–2016), an early advocate for inclusivity in design, it "doesn't mean you're designing one thing for all people. You're designing a diversity of ways to participate so everyone has a sense of belonging." Through observation and testing our preconceived ideas about how a space can function, we can aim to make designs that flatten ideas of limited access and hierarchies of function.

In the United Kingdom, the Design Council (previously known as The Commission for Architecture and the Built Environment or "CABE"), raises awareness of the need for designing inclusive environments for diverse users of a space. The Design Council's principles of inclusive design, which they outline as being welcoming to everyone, call for design that is responsive to people's needs; intuitive to use; flexible enough to offer choices when a single design solution cannot meet all user needs; convenient without involving undue effort or special separation, or limiting independence.

Designers must anticipate the diverse range of users of a space and design with those principles. Involving potential users at all stages of the design process is an easy method for gaining consensus. As no one space or piece of furniture will be used in the same way by everyone, designers should instead offer users choices as an agent of empowerment.

The Hazelwood School in Glasgow is a school for "dual sensory impaired" students, meaning students who are blind and deaf. The architecture and interiors by Alan Dunlop Architect Limited respond to that need with the incorporation of supportive, sensory guides and safe materials that empower the students to move independently and comfortably throughout the space.

The Stalled! project by architect Joel Sanders, transgender historian Susan Stryker, and legal scholar Terry Kogan "treats restrooms as a means to generate a larger conversation about the relationship between environmental design, the human body and social equity."

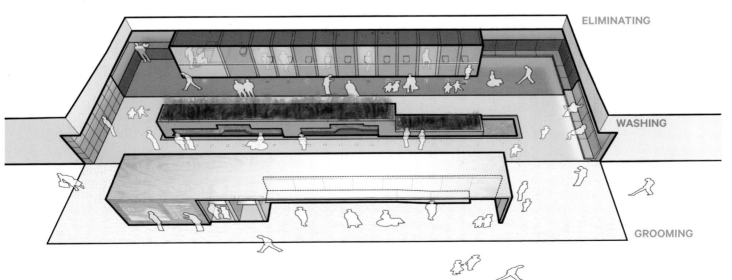

ELIMINATING

WASHING

GROOMING

49 Innovation

The use of transformative methods and solutions to improve a design.

See Also
Creativity
Discovery
Inspiration
Technology

Innovation in interior design is the development of a new idea or method that makes implementing a solution better, easier, and more efficient. Being innovative requires a designer to examine a problem from all sides, and to develop solutions that challenge our traditional response to it.

The process of developing innovative responses to a design challenge is solution-based, not problem-based. The issues surrounding the design of interior spaces have not changed much over the course of the profession's short history, but with increasing engagement and interactions with clients, consumers, and end users, designers can develop a more comprehensive solution to a design brief. Innovation occurs through the generation of ideas, the production of prototypes, and the subsequent testing—and failure—that leads to refinements and improvements to the solution.

Innovation can occur at all scales in an interior design project. These investigations into transformative models can be as practical as making a space more usable, or can engage in a holistic view of project delivery and scheduling.

Areas for Design Innovation
Accessibility
Aesthetics
Capacity
Differentiation
Durability
Efficiency
Engagement
Environments
Experience
Integration
Modularity
Performance
Productivity
Quality
Reliability
Technology
Safety
Structure
Sustainability
Usability

This hyperbolic paraboloid ceiling at the Daniels Faculty of Architecture, Landscape and Design at the University of Toronto, was prototyped and developed by Boston-based NADAAA by exploring how simple metal framing and thin gypsum-covered plywood can create an exceptional space.

A retractable staircase and an under-the-loft-bed alcove desk are the innovative features in this micro-hotel suite for Zoku in Amsterdam, the Netherlands, by Dutch design studio Concrete.

Breakthroughs in biotechnology are advancing the way materials are produced. Forager hides, by Ecovative, are a sustainable vegan leather grown from mycelium, a carefully selected specific species of mushrooms.

50 Inspiration

An influence or agent to spark creativity.

See Also
Design Process
Discovery
Technology

Design projects often begin with a spark, an idea, or a moment of inspiration. Starting a project can be intimidating—like a blank piece of paper or a screen waiting for input—and a designer needs an expansive look at the where and how to begin. Whether it is the design of a product, the renovation of a room, or the reinvention of an entire building, there is typically something catalytic that serves as the impetus for an idea about how to move from inspiration to action. Examples may include a specific article of clothing, a type of flower, a specific era to strike a tone or mood, or a color or group of colors found in an abstract painting.

The origins of the English word "inspire" dates back to the fourteenth century, with the Latin root *inspirare*, which means "to breathe or blow into or upon." With our interconnected world, we are no longer restricted to print media or our immediate environment when we look for inspiration. The advent of sharing platforms has made the entirety of design's history available to us, which simultaneously opens the designer to a wide range of influences but also overwhelms with too many to choose from. Having a discerning eye for the cyclical nature of what is considered beautiful and "of the moment" requires a designer to maintain an active curiosity and openness to the world around them.

Inspiration is often the basis for selecting the theme, colors, patterns, and textures in a design project. There are many websites and services that serve as aggregators and storage for image collection. Subscriptions to design and culture magazines and journals can provide a reusable wealth of sources, and building a library of books and monographs should be the envy of every designer's office and studio.

Belgian designer Sylvain Willenz took inspiration from camouflaged naval ships from the early 1900s for the op-art design of the *Razzle Dazzle* textile collection for Febrik/Kvadrat.

Memphis Group furniture of the 1980s—known for its bold colors, euclidean geometric forms, and energetic patterns—inspired the design of the Ya Space! furniture showroom by PIG Design in Hangzhou, China.

51 Layering

The overlapping of elements in space.

See Also
Finishes
Materiality
Styling
Texture

The principle of layering uses overlap and aggregation to develop more sophisticated solutions that resonate in a design. Layers can be both vertical and horizontal planes, or can be dimensional objects that cover or obscure each other visually to create a more complex composition.

A designer works with layers by treating each space as a blank canvas, and layering occurs in many design strategies and solutions. It is a spatial idea in addition to the two-dimensional overlapping of elements such as flooring and wallcoverings. Moving objects closer together can make spaces appear cozier, and having fewer layered spaces has an lightness to a rooms appearance.

A designer works with layers by treating each space as a blank canvas, examining the surfaces that make up the room and making decisions about their hierarchy and identity in a place. By adding objects against that established background, fixtures such as built-in millwork and larger furniture set the tone of the space and suggest movement through it. Smaller objects, artworks, and textures further strengthen the sense of depth that layering provides.

Views through rooms can also emphasize layering, with doors, windows, and other openings acting as a layering of volumes, which can emphasize contrasting light and dark tones. They can also appear closely linked through the use of similar materials and complementary furnishings.

Floor coverings, furniture, lighting, and natural elements overlap in this rendering from Spacejoy, an online interior design service.

An apartment in Moscow by Blockstudio utilizes furniture, light fixtures, and transparent surfaces to create an overlap of spaces and uses.

Designed by the Huntsman Architectural Group, the large, open room of the advertising agency Argonaut layers new furnishings within a historic setting. the design layers materials within a similar contrasting color palette, which emphasizes the unique quality of the space.

52 Lighting

The use of light to illuminate and enhance the experience of an interior space.

See Also
Character
Detail
Mood
Natural Lighting

Lighting is essential to the experience of a space. Illumination sets a mood, makes tasks easier to perform, and make spaces more accessible. Interior designers use light fixtures of all types—ceiling, pendant, floor, uplights, and feature lights—to address specific purposes and needs.

The design of a lighting system, which can be broken down into ambient, task, and accent lighting, is an expertise that occasionally warrants the use of a professional light designer. However in most cases, lighting solutions can be developed by the designer through light simulations, and by referencing the recommendations of the various professional organizations that provide rules of thumb to follow.

Advanced light simulations allow for the designer to check a desired lighting effect prior to finalizing plans and documents, and many technologies exist for controlling and programming light based on time of day and desired scenes.

The Illuminating Engineering Society (www.ies.org) publishes the Lighting Library, a subscription source that provides access to lighting science, practice, and applications, as well as measurements and testing.

Foot Candle
A somewhat archaic metric, a foot candle refers to the amount of light that hits an adjacent surface, and is measured by the standard of one lumen of light at a one-foot (25 cm) distance.

Lumen
The unit of measure that describes the luminous flux or useful light emitted by a source of light.

Color Temperature
The measurement in kelvins of how warm (yellow) or cool (blue) the hue of a light source is.

Designed by Stephan Braunfels, the café in the Paul Löbe House in Berlin, Germany uses multiple colored-glass light fixtures to animate the ceiling plane.

A corridor at FC Barcelona's Camp Nou is washed with high-intensity color.

Interior designers can choose from these different types of lighting to create the lighting plan of a space

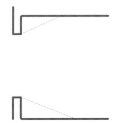

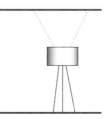

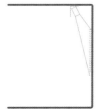

General Illumination
The amount of ambient light in a space.

Downlighting
Specific task and work plane illumination.

Uplighting
Highlights elements from below; can be moved if a standing floor lamp.

Backlighting
Used to create luminous surfaces and enhance the sense of depth in a space.

Feature Lighting
Specific light on an object or work of art.

Accent Lighting
Similar to feature lighting; used to illuminate the path or circulation through a space.

53 Line

A vector that connects two points in space.

See Also
Movement
Organic
Red Thread
Sight Lines

Lines exist in every aspect and process of interior design. It is what we use when we begin a project; when aggregated, it becomes how we describe intent; when expressed as a curve, it implies the tracing of movement or touch; and when marked on a surface, it becomes an element of division. Lines can be inherent to an object—a board and batten wall system, or a fluted column—or applied to a surface—an etched line on a metal panel, the line dividing paint colors and finishes. Regardless, lines can have an outsized impact on how a space is perceived and used.

As inherently two-dimensional elements, lines can affect a room or space depending on their orientation, direction, and placement. Lines used vertically imply strength, as though something is being supported. The vertical thrust and repetition of linear elements can have the visual illusion of increasing the height of a room. Horizontal lines placed on walls and objects can add a perception of weight, of stability. They imply direction, and create the illusion of adding width to a space. The imposition of diagonal lines suggests movement and dynamic action, and based on direction, can lead the eye either up or down. Diagonal lines do not have to hold onto corners; they can begin and end at any point above or below the midpoint of a surface. The curve is a defined path between two points, an inscription of organic and freeform shape. The application of a line as a curve can imply motion; yet curves, and curved surfaces, are some of the most challenging elements to use in an interior.

Strong vertical lines combined with dynamic lighting organize and add visual interest to this lounge.

Universal Principles of Interior Design

In the École Jean Macé Pavillons sous Bois, Atelier 2A+ Architecture installed Mosa tiles to implement lines that provide visual cues for use.

The interior volume in the Olso Opera House by Snøhetta is clad in varying depth of wood that catch the linear qualities of light and shadow.

54 Materiality

The character and quality of matter.

See Also
Craft
Connection
Surface
Texture

Materials are the essence of an interior. An interior is essentially a collection of material surfaces in relation to each other. Materials set the tone of an interior, affect the quality of light in a space, determine how a room sounds, and influence our perception of depth and height.

The interior design profession has a complex relationship with materials. Some materials are integral to their source (stone, wood), others are composites that still have volume (ceramics, some plastics, and solid surfaces) and finally, some are applied directly or indirectly as surfaces (wallpaper, paint, foils, and graphics). All have a place in the composition of a project, and can have resonance with a designer's vision. Materials also have emotional associations to a place and history, and can add compelling narratives to a design.

Materials aggregate in a space, creating patterns and vibrant surfaces, or can soothe through the use of large expanses. Materiality is closely related to the other design principles of craft and connection. The feel of a surface can resonate with a hand's touch, provide color to a space, and affect how sounds resonate (i.e., acoustics).

Maison Luis Carré, a residence in Bazoches, France, by the architect and design Alvar Aalto, is an exquisite lesson in the use of materials that are integral to the design and intimate to the touch.

A *washitsu* room (often referred to as a "tatami room" in Western culture) is measured based on the material dimensions of a mat, whose natural fibers resonate with the natural palette of the room.

In the Milan hotel Room Mate Giulia, the designer Patricia Urquiola uses a whimsical palette of color as well as multiple materials that enhance the welcoming character of the space.

55 Measurement

The quantification of length, width, height, or volume.

See Also
Ratio
Shape
Surface
Volume

Closely related to scale, measurement is an essential part of communicating design intent, ensuring compliance with clearances, and adhering to code requirements. The ability to quantify an object using a common system of measure has been with humanity since the early measurement systems of Mesopotamia and Egypt, to the development of the Roman *pes* (or Roman foot), which was imported to England in the mid 1600s. Two main systems of measurement—the imperial system (feet and inches) and the metric system (meters and centimeters, also known as the International System of Units or SI)—are dominant in our contemporary world, and are the basis for measurement in design.

The imperial system was formalized in England in the 1820s with the adoption of the Weights and Measures Act, when all other methods of measurement were repealed. In this system, the units of inch, foot, yard, and mile are used to determine length, with area and volume measurements referred to as squared and cubed respectively.

The metric system of measurement was developed in France after the French Revolution of 1789–99. It is based on the unit of one meter, which was estimated to be one ten-millionth of the distance from the geographic North Pole to the equator, measured over the earth's surface along a meridian running through Paris, France. The ease of use of metric, which is based on a powers of ten system, has made the International System of Units (or SI) the dominant system of measurement in the world. Length is indicated using the millimeter, centimeter, meter, and kilometer.

Measurement seem intuitive, yet it informs many decisions in the design process both aesthetically and legally. From the mundane (the ideal distance from a chair to a table), to the specific (the width of corridors and doors, or the height of a counter), measurements affect every aspect of an interior.

The public standards of length (in yards and feet) at the Royal Observatory, in Greenwich, England.

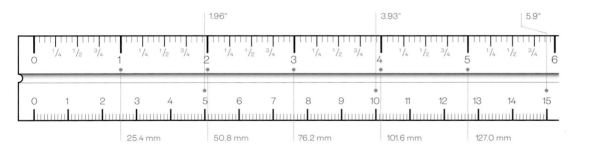

Metric and imperial measurements and translations.

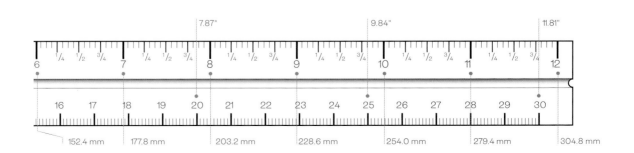

56 Modeling

The use of computational tools to document and visualize an interior space.

See Also
Design Process
Form
Lighting
Representation

Three-dimensional modeling and rendering is one of the most critical tools in a designer's toolkit. The ability to easily and accurately dimension a space, and choose vantage points from which to view and make design decisions can ensure the success of a project.

Deciding on the appropriate software to invest in is a complex issue that designers will need to address. Some design programs offer an ease of use that might be beneficial in the early stages of a project. Others allow for the full integration of a building project, with the ability to create plans, sections, elevations, and complete three-dimensional representations. As with other types of software, a significant amount of time needs to be invested in order to develop the appropriate skills.

More recent developments in hardware enable projects to be represented in real time, giving designers the ability to make decisions about materials and lighting effects, as well as help with presentations to clients. In addition, the ability to render soft materials, access the extensive libraries of three-dimensional models from furniture manufacturers, and use sites that offer realistic images and descriptions of materials, vegetation, and other objects make the design decision-making process more effective.

By enabling precision in placement and visualization, a dimensionally accurate model can aid in the pricing and estimating of a project. More advanced tools can look at the effects of daylight and perform energy analysis. These advanced applications can help reduce the use of certain materials, and make the project more energy- and cost-efficient.

Further Resources

Although the choice of tools to use for three-dimensional modeling is constantly evolving, the list below is a good start, but check the general websites for the most recent versions of software.

Render
D5 Render www.d5render.com
Twinmotion www.unrealengine.com
Maxwell Render maxwellrender.com
Arnold www.arnoldrenderer.com
Enscape enscape3d.com
Cycles www.blender.org

Model/Render
Blender www.blender.org
SketchUp Pro www.sketchup.com
3ds Max www.autodesk.com/products/3ds-max
Homestyler www.homestyler.com

Model/Render/Document
Archicad graphisoft.com
Vectorworks www.vectorworks.net
Revit and AutoCAD www.autodesk.com

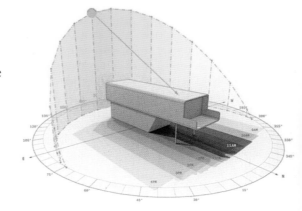

An example of a model that can evaluate the energy needs of a project via solar analysis.

Advanced renderings of interiors can be produced using open-source applications, such as Blender.

Building Information Models contain all of the information needed to document a project—plans, sections, material, and furniture schedules.

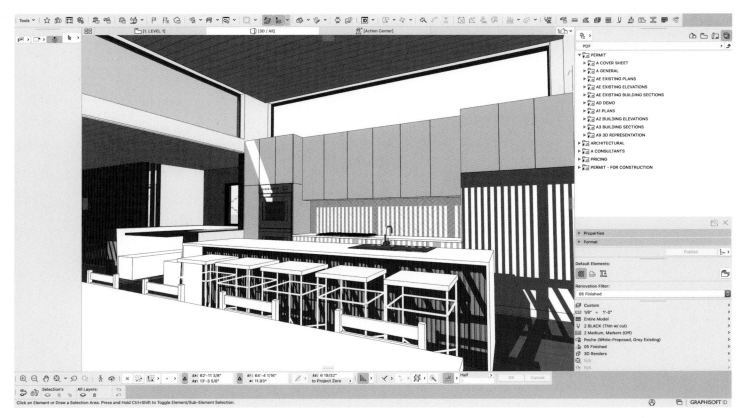

57 Modularity

A system made up of standardized units or dimensions characterized by flexibility or variety in function.

See Also
Adaptability
Connection
Function
Innovation

Modularity exists at all scales of the design process. It's a standardized system that allows for more efficient fabrication, production, and application. It is extremely beneficial to the product industry as the assembly process speeds up; it also saves money in shipping because modular units can be broken down to smaller pieces (flat-packed) and more easily assembled by the user. Examples of modular systems include the joy of Lego sets, IKEA's self-assembled systems, Japanese tatami mats that determine the dimensions of a room, and prefabricated wall systems, furniture, and housing.

Components of a design may be separated and recombined, which allows for flexibility and variety in function. This design approach works with smaller parts that can be stacked, customized, rearranged, and reused. In addition, modular systems are inherently sustainable, with the option to change or retrofit modules without replacing an entire system.

Built from 140 self-contained prefabricated apartment capsules in 1972, the Nagakin Capsule Tower in Tokyo (designed by Kisho Kurokawa) was one of the first large-scale architecture projects to use modular parts both inside and out. The interiors of each capsule contained modular built-in cabinets, appliances, plumbing fixtures, and furnishings.

Designed by Danish architecture firm BIG, the Voxel sofa system for Common Seating was inspired by Legos, Minecraft, and the architecture of Mies van der Rohe, all of which use grid systems and modular building blocks. The adaptable seating collection can be configured into multiple seating scenarios, as a space's programmatic needs change or evolve.

Pair's Olli system is a contemporary modular workplace solution that adapts to users' needs.

58 Monochrome

A single color or hue that acts as the dominant color theme within a space.

See Also
Color Scheme
Hue
Materiality
Tone

Further Reading
Shoko Wanger, "How to Pull Off a Monochromatic Room," *Architectural Digest*, May 25, 2017, www.architecturaldigest.com/story/monochromatic-room-design-tips.

Monochrome refers to designing in one color or in the same undertones. Monochromatic color schemes are derived from a single base hue and are extended using variations of its tints, shades, and tones. Monochromatic interiors can also be accented and enhanced by architectural features, materials, textures, and art.

Designing with a monochrome palette can create a sense of calm and reduce visual clutter. This is supported by the mechanics of how the eye perceives images. Due to the processing of light in the human retina, it is easier for the human brain to detect a single wavelength of color rather than a range of wavelengths from multiple color families. Repeating color makes a space simpler to process and as a result, it looks more comfortable and aesthetically soothing. By avoiding contrasting colors, and using a monochromatic color scheme, designers create spaces that are more comfortable for people with color blindness.

Hue
Hue is the base color and serves as the foundation of the overall color scheme. Hue must be carefully considered, as it will set the mood of a space.

Tint
Tint is a lighter version of the hue and is the basic color with white added.

Shade
Shade is a darker version of the hue that acts as a contrast to the base color, and is essentially the hue with black added.

Tone
Similar to shade, tone is a darker version of the hue but with grey added. This results in a less bright and more muted appearance.

Designed by local studio Onion, the furniture and surfaces in a Bangkok, Thailand, eatery are made exclusively from ash and plywood. Even the pendant lamps and awnings, commonly found in outdoor street stalls, are built in monochromatic wood.

Texture

Texture becomes more important when designing with a monochromatic palette. Variations in textures will keep the color from appearing too flat.

The renovation of the historic civic building Felix Meritis in Amsterdam by i29 incorporates monochromatic greens into the custom tapestry-like walls, furniture, and flooring.

59 Mood

The use of materials, furnishings, and color to evoke emotion.

See Also
Character
Contrast
Layering
Storytelling

A mood is the establishment of a set of ideas that are based on color, furniture style, lighting, and textures. A mood is typically developed early in the design process, and represents the direction for the palette of materials and furnishings that will be used during the development of an interior's design.

Mood boards, or the art of collecting inspiration, materials, and themes together, have evolved over the relatively short history of interior design. In the late twentieth century, interior designers presented physical sample boards to clients, with actual materials hot-glued to a board for presentation. Ideally, materials should be proportionally represented on the board to give the client a clear understanding of the ambience, fixtures, furniture, and finishes that comprise the elements of a design proposal. With the arrival of the Internet, the ability to gather and share images and ideas with clients and collaborators has shifted to mostly digital boards and sites that cater to the collection and arrangement of ideas.

If the space of a project is existing, a designer can look to the proportion of the space, the size of openings and windows, orientation, and context as a beginning point to create a mood. For example, a house by the ocean suggests an open, airy, and light-filled space, with cool tones and lighter hues that reflect and bounce the color of the sea into the rooms.

Once materials are gathered, the interior designer can use informal arrangements to begin to explore combinations of texture and color.

In the Minerals Gallery at London's Museum of Natural History, heavy casework and rusticated columns establish a subdued atmosphere that suggests study and quiet conversation.

There are several digital tools and apps that can be used to create mood boards. Slide sharing and online collaboration tools make communicating ideas easy and efficient. In addition, websites such as MaterialBank provide designers with access to a multitude of samples from a number of sources.

Presentation Tools
For developing narrative-based mood boards
Google Slides www.slides.google.com
PowerPoint www.microsoft.com
Keynote www.apple.com/keynote

Collaboration Tools
For developing collaborative and interactive mood boards
Miro www.miro.com
Pinterest www.pinterest.com

Material Samples
MaterialBank www.materialbank.com

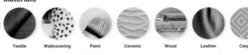

60 Movement

The quality in design that represents or suggests motion.

See Also
Connection
Form
Line
Texture
Volume

Motion is the change of position over time of an object or body, but movement is the quality that represents a suggested motion. Understanding the principle of movement might be easier to think of in terms of two-dimensional pieces, such as an artwork. Artists often use forms and colors to imply movement and guide the viewer's eye in, through, along, and out of a composition. Lines, forms, and shapes can affect the pace, direction, and legibility of movement.

A three-dimensional volume offers the development of a more complex narrative. In a room, the composition of elements can move the viewer's eye through the space, often to a focal point or focal area. In some cases, movement in a design describes the quality of the physical motion or circulation of the user across a hallway, up a staircase, or through a series of rooms. For example, visitors tend to move contemplatively through a museum or gallery, but circulate more purposefully in a gym or health center.

Tied closely to rhythm, movement in interiors can be achieved by repetitive design elements such as lines, textures, colors, and patterns. The incorporation of movement into a design solution will ultimately lead to a more dynamic experience of a space.

Katsushika Hokusai's woodblock print *The Great Wave off Kanagawa* (1823) is an example of composition that explores movement. The curved forms of the waves and mountains tend to move the viewer's eye across the artwork from the wave on the left, along the boats, to the mountain, and out to the right.

Drew Mandel's use of sinuous lines and continuous surfaces in this staircase emphasize the vertical movement through this contemporary addition to a house in Toronto, Canada.

This sushi restaurant by BOS|UA uses Hokusai's print as a mural wall.

61 Natural Lighting

The use of direct and ambient light from the sun in a space.

See Also
Character
Lighting
Orientation
Sustainability

As one of the most important considerations in the design process, natural light has psychological and physiological effects on the wellness of users. Also known as *daylighting*, this design technique efficiently brings natural light into a space using exterior glazing, windows, doors, and skylights. Such strategies also can save energy by reducing the need for artificial lighting.

In addition, fixtures, paint, and finishes can increase or decrease the reflectivity of the natural light, which bounces throughout a space until all of its energy is absorbed. The science of daylighting design is complex; when choosing a daylight fixture, a designer must consider balancing heat gains and losses, reducing glare, and controlling the variations in availability of daylight.

This coworking space in London is flooded with diffuse natural light from large exterior windows. Additional internal glazing brings light deep into the other rooms.

Natural Light Reflection

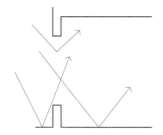

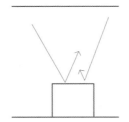

External Reflection
Light that reflects off ground surfaces, adjacent buildings, window sills, and light shelves. (Excessive reflection can cause glare and may be undesirable).

Internal Reflection
Light reflecting off internal walls, ceilings, and floors; includes highly reflective surfaces (smooth or glossy), and white or light finishes and mirrors.

Universal Principles of Interior Design

The Liberation Coffee House by ORA located in the Los Angeles LGBT Center uses a colorful array of blinds to diffuse the intensity of the California sun.

Daylighting Fixtures

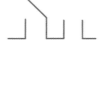

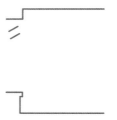

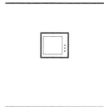

Windows
Most common source of daylight.

Skylights
Provide lighting from above, and can be passive or active.

Solar Tubes
Light channels that allow light to enter from roof and reflected with mirrors.

Redirection Devices
Direct incoming sunlight to ceiling; reduce glare and increase daylight penetration.

Solar Shading Devices
Include blinds and overhangs to control solar gains and glare from windows.

Electric Lighting Controls
Incorporate photocell sensors to dim or turn off a lighting system in response to available light.

62 Occupancy

The type of use and number of occupants that is permitted in a space.

See Also
Adjacency
Codes
Health, Safety,
and Welfare
Program

Reference
*International Building
Code, Chapter 3, Use
and Occupancy Classi-
fication.

In the simplest terms, the occupant load of buildings, or areas within buildings are based on the size, function, and location, as well as by local health and safety requirements. In the U.S., this classification is determined by the International Building Code (IBC) but may vary by country or municipality based on their regulations.

This classification is based on the function of a space and includes the following groups Assembly (A), Business (B), Educational (E), Factory and Industrial (F), High Hazard (H), Institutional (I), Mercantile (M), Residential (R), Storage (S), and Utility and Miscellaneous (U).*

Occupancy loads are developed with the goal of protecting people in buildings from the presence of a fire. They also provide guidelines for sprinkler location and egress requirements. An interior designer should understand occupancy constraints and design accordingly, whether it concerns positioning of partitions, furniture layouts, or coordination with lighting and electrical contractors.

In any rooms or spaces qualified as assembly for gathering purposes, the occupant load must be clearly posted in a visible location near the main exit. This sign may be referenced during periodic inspection by the fire marshal or building officials.

The area of an interior and its intended use dictate the number of occupants that are allowed at any given time.

The Lawrenceville School Gruss Center for Art and Design in New Jersey by Sasaki transforms a simple stairwell into a gathering place and also inserts seating into the underside of the stairwell.

The Metropolitan Opera House in New York as seen in 1937. Occupancy loads are developed to protect the inhabitants of a building.

63 Organic

Forms related to or derived from nature in interior design.

See Also
Biomimicry
Form
Shape
Volume

Organic forms in interior design are developed in a number of ways—whether they are the natural elements that comprise a material, the inclusion of living elements, or the use of organic shapes and furnishings rather than the more traditional rectilinear walls and floors of typical construction.

Curves and shapes derived from nature, when used carefully, can soften a space, ease transitions from one room to another, and make changes in light more subtle and ephemeral. Curved walls, radius corners, soft furniture forms, and flowing light fixtures are all elements that can be combined in a complete scheme; or they can be added to a rectilinear space to offset rigid lines and severe spaces.

Organic plans and sections require a level of sophistication and coordination that is hard to achieve. In construction and implementation, organic details have to be carefully thought through and coordinated, and a high level of craft is needed to make the finishes as smooth as the forms themselves.

Curved linear plates stack to create this dramatic library in Binhai, China, designed by MVRDV.

The main atrium and circulation space of Calgary's new Central Library by Snøhetta uses organic forms and materials in its design.

The Cloverleaf sofa, designed by Verner Panton in 1969 for Verpan, uses organic lines to allow for both modularity and multisided use.

64 Orientation

The positioning, placement, or arrangement of elements depending on the position of the sun.

See Also
Natural Lighting
Placement
Wayfinding
Zones

Orientation, derived from the Latin word *orientum,* meaning "the rising sun," refers to the position of a building relative to the sun. In ancient Egypt, Mesopotamia, and Central America, the entrances and passages of important buildings faced east, in the direction of the rising sun. Orientation also varies according to religious considerations Muslims turn toward Mecca, which is whatever direction that might be from where they are at that moment. While the Old St. Peter's Basilica was oriented to the west, later Christian churches (or their altars) faced the east.

With sustainability in mind, building orientation is an important part of the design process. Good building orientation maximizes natural light and ventilation in all climates and seasons, ensuring climatic comfort within the building, saving on energy costs, and offsetting the negative impacts of inclement weather and climate change. A design should take maximum advantage of both daily and seasonal variations of the sun's radiation.

Solar Orientation Radiation intensity depends on the direction of the sun's rays, increasing or decreasing building temperatures.

Wind Orientation To create natural ventilation, windows and doors should be located to take advantage of the prevailing wind patterns.

Although it's not always possible to control the siting of a building, interior designers can strategically position rooms and their components (such as window shades or blinds, furniture, or plants) relative to where sunlight enters the space.

The Capilano Library by Patkau Architects in Edmonton, Canada, utilizes the site to develop access to light and, through sectional volumes, zones the spaces of the library.

65 Pattern

The repetition of a geometric graphic on a surface.

See Also Grid
Rhythm
Scale
Texture

A pattern is made by the repetition of elements, typically arranged on a grid, that generates order and a sense of rhythm, and that can help create textures and surface elements, or add organization to a design.

Patterns provide visual interest to surfaces in a space in elements such as flooring, textiles, and wall coverings. Patterns can also be found in the aggregation of finishes, the repetition of cabinetry, or in the detailing of walls and floors.

In upholstery, pattern can add visual texture depending on the techniques by which they are woven. Color combinations also influence the intensity of a pattern, the more contrasting and complementary, the more dynamic the visual and graphic presence, while patterns developed through the use of similar tones will have a more subtle appearance. A small amount of pattern can be utilized to highlight a special feature of a room; when used comprehensively, pattern can unite a space.

Designers should understand the effects of patterned surface on an interior. Consider the size and style of space before injecting patterns. Be mindful of the size and directionality of patterns.

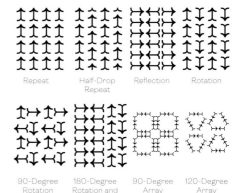

Repeat   Half-Drop   Reflection   Rotation
          Repeat

90-Degree   180-Degree   90-Degree   120-Degree
Rotation   Rotation and Array   Array
             Reflection

The repetition of pattern in a design, known as a "pattern repeat," can be mirrored, shifted, or rotated to develop different effects.

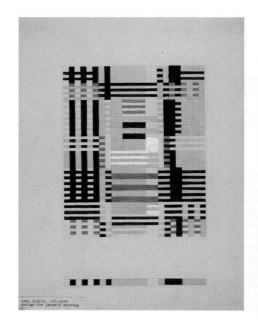

The pattern for Anni Albers's *Design for a Jacquard Weaving* uses bold, overlapping lines and colors.

Mario Botta's bold use of graphic pattern is integral to the floors, walls, and architecture of San Giovanni Battista church in Mogno, Switzerland.

Finding inspiration in the patterns of the urban environment, the UP collection by Kelly Harris Smith for HBF Textiles incorporates a wide range of hues and scales.

66 Perspective

The three-dimensional representation of an image or space.

See Also
Composition
Grid
Line
Modeling

The development of a method of linear perspective was critical to the advancement of art and design practices. In essence, it was a technique to render objects relative to the space they occupy. Although credit is typically given to architect Filippo Brunelleschi (1377—1446), the discovery of the vanishing point (or points) to which parallel lines converge can also be traced back to the primitive use of stacking and layering, the oblique projections of early Chinese illustrations (particularly the *dengjia toushi* method), and Japanese art. These explorations led to a revolution in the representational art of the Renaissance, and its use as a communication medium for architects and designers.

Three-dimensional drawings are used in interior design projects to demonstrate aspects of the design that cannot be readily understood through two-dimensional representations. They can demonstrate and explain many aspects of a project, such as furniture details, color, finish, light, and shadow.

While mechanical perspective construction has been overtaken by computer-aided design, the underlying foundations of perspective representation remain a point of view (the eye point), an imagined picture plane into which the image is projected, a horizon line (eye level), and a vanishing point. With the emergence of virtual reality (VR) headsets and real time rendering engines, the problematic aspects of having a static point of view are largely overcome.

An illustration from *Romance of the Three Kingdoms*, Chinese, c. fifteenth century.

Although constructed perspectives are used less frequently, the main principles still apply. The Vanishing Point (**VP**), Horizon Line (**HL**), and Picture Plane (**PP**) are all relevant to framing and point of view.

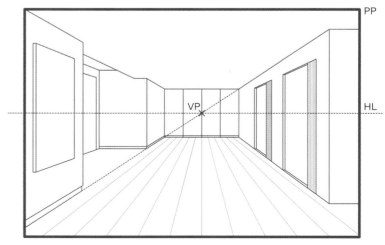

Perspective views
are necessary in all
representations and
phases of a project,
from photography
(such as this photo
of the renovation of
the Johnson Building
at the Boston Public
Library by William
Rawn Associates), to
interiors and sketches
(like this rendering
of a community arts
center in Somerville by
OverUnder).

67 Philosophy

A particular set of ideas about knowledge, truth, and the nature and meaning of life. In design, a set of guiding principles and intentions.

See Also
Harmony
Preservation
Regionalism
Storytelling

How do designers create spaces that are both beautiful and useful? Where do they find inspiration? Do they follow set rules or guidelines, or their own instincts?

Philosophies of design are an effective way to improve well-being and reduce anxiety of the user by following a set of rules that guide design decisions. While cultural influences and traditions have developed regional philosophies, some designers develop their own philosophies and intentions after years of experience practicing them consistently from project to project.

The phrase "less is more," often mistakenly attributed to the architect Mies van der Rohe—but initially coined by his mentor, Peter Behrens—refers to the Modernist ethic of designing with simple forms and distilling elements to only what is necessary, and can be characterized by the simplicity of tectonic expression and the austerity of materials and space. Another famous aphorism, "form follows function," was developed by architects in Chicago at the turn of the twentieth century, and valued usability over aesthetics, and that a space should clearly be designed with its intended purpose in mind.

Hygge
Danish, refers to simple enjoyment, intentional coziness, items that create serenity, cozy blankets, candles, comfy pillows, making space for unwinding/relaxing, use of natural materials like wood and wool.

Feng Shui
Ancient Chinese practice (which means "wind-water" in English) that involves the positioning of objects to achieve harmony, support good energy "qi" and patterns of yin and yang energy. Wind and light must move well, spaces should be without clutter, and energy flow should be considered (e.g., mirrors reflect energy). The five elements (wood, earth, metal, fire, and water) should be included in every room.

Wabi Sabi
Japanese ethos from the fifteenth century that focuses on simple pleasures, authentic materials, and finding beauty in imperfection. Design spaces with a sense of peace and tranquility by using natural materials like stone, concrete, wood, woven rugs, and handmade textiles.

Lagom
Swedish/Norwegian expression that means "just the right amount"—not too much, not too little, in moderation, finding balance in having the right amount, practicing mindfulness with possessions, decluttering by getting rid of objects that are no longer useful. Upcycling, recycling, and using sustainable materials. Wood burning and wood as environmentally friendly fuel.

The interior aesthetic of Tokyo restaurant Grillno is defined by simplicity and minimalism.

A Hong Kong residence by Nelson Chow was designed with wabi sabi to be beautiful and functional, and is built with bronze that is meant to age gracefully.

68 Placement

The act of putting something in a particular point in space.

See Also
Alignment
Asymmetry
Balance
Emphasis

The placement of objects in a space is driven by program, adjacency, function, and orientation. Although it is often not possible to control the siting of an interior, designers can strategically choose the placement of program and its components depending on the orientation to daylight, access to circulation, or proximity to openings and apertures.

At the room level, placement strategies affect circulation, acoustics, and fixture location. Plans can be developed through schemes that include arranging elements at the perimeter of a room or symmetrically at the center, choosing the placement of clusters and groupings, and balancing open space with functional needs.

At Momofuku Las Vegas, booths and tables for larger gatherings are placed near the perimeter of the space, while more intimate groupings are arranged in the center.

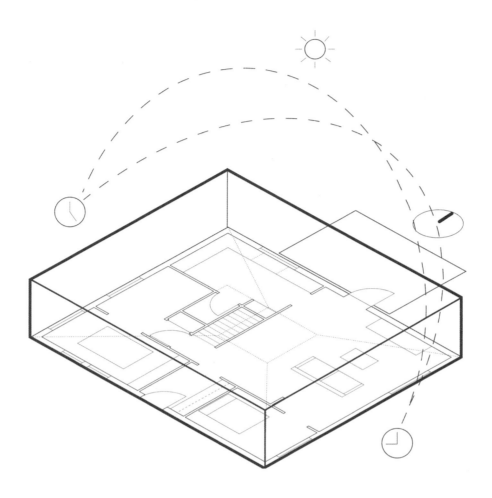

North-Facing Rooms

Types Living room, family room, dining room, outdoor living spaces.

Characteristics Good daylight most of day, solar gain most of day throughout year, likely require horizontal shading to prevent overheating, good solar gain in winter.

East-Facing Rooms

Types Kitchen, breakfast.

Characteristics Early morning light, solar gain throughout the year, cooler in late afternoon, good morning light.

West-Facing Rooms

Types Living areas.

Characteristics Good afternoon daylight, potential to overheat in late afternoon, may require vertical shading to prevent glare or overheating, provides good solar gain for thermal mass heating.

South-Facing Rooms

Types Less habitable spaces, garage, laundry, bathroom, workroom, stairs.

Characteristics Lower levels of daylight during parts of the year, little to no heat gain.

69 Preservation

The act of restoring a space through the identification of elements and characteristics deemed historically important.

See Also
Adaptability
Durability
Social Impact
Sustainability

When renovating or restoring interiors, it is important to recognize the elements that are important to their history. Any significant work of architecture and design that is fifty years old (which is the threshold for many nations) meets the criteria for designation as an historic structure. Structures younger than fifty can be designated historic but need more consideration for designation.

Historic spaces also have cultural resonance and tell compelling narratives, but spaces that have been preserved often represent the dominant culture. In the last decade, it has become essential in preservation to acknowledge a more inclusive and diverse definition of what should be saved and restored. Making such meaningful decisions can be accomplished by expanding the voices that are included in the conversations about preservation that expand our understanding of what makes our communities unique and memorable.

There are several organizations, agencies, and activist groups that work from global to local scales and at all varieties of building types. In addition, there are tax incentives that can offset the significant cost of restoring and preserving buildings and interiors.

The demolition of Grand Central Station (which began in 1963) was seen as an act of cultural vandalism, and saw the establishment of the Landmarks Preservation Commission in the city of New York.

United Nations
Educational, Scientific and
Cultural Organization

Docomomo
A nonprofit organization founded in 1988 dedicated to the documentation and conservation of buildings, sites, and neighborhoods of the Modern Movement. There are national chapters that advocate on behalf of modern buildings.

National Trust for Historic Preservation
Another nonprofit, U.S.-based organization that has for seventy years led the movement to save America's historic places.

World Heritage Sites
The United Nations Educational, Scientific, and Cultural Organization (UNESCO) seeks to encourage the identification, protection, and preservation of cultural and natural heritage considered to be of outstanding value to humanity around the world.

The Museum Hotel Antakya in Turkey is located on a site of ancient Roman ruins that were discovered after the project started.

The iconic TWA Flight Center, designed by Eero Saarinen in 1962, was meticulously restored by Beyer Blinder Belle and transformed into a hotel according to the Secretary of the Interior's Standards for Restoration, working closely with the New York State Historic Preservation Office.

70 Program

The definition of the needs and functions in a design.

See Also
Design Process
Function
Occupancy
Zones

Often referred to as the "predesign" phase of a project, determining the program is a crucial part of the design process. Whether for a large commercial project or a home kitchen renovation, this phase allows the designer to examine the functional performance, constraints, and opportunities of a project.

The program should clearly define what spaces, features, or attributes must be added to improve functionality, work together efficiently, meet the needs of the client, and begin to define an appropriate and compelling character for a space.

It is critical to the design process in order for the constraints, spatial adjacencies, and design objectives of a project to be clearly defined and documented. Throughout the project, the program should serve as a foundation for all who are involved to reference in subsequent phases.

The programming process can be broken down into three fundamental types of activities researching, analyzing, and documenting information. Within this framework, the process for determining the program can vary widely, depending on type and scope of project.

Research
✓ Collect plans and drawings.
✓ Visit site with client.
✓ Report field observations.
✓ Determine client organization and end users.
✓ Review any building codes and zoning regulations.
✓ Interview client representatives and end users.
✓ Compile information on client (mission, structure, goals).

Analyze
✓ Analyze interview notes.
✓ Create diagrams of ideal spatial relationships.
✓ Determine occupancy counts and future projections, consultants, or other professionals needed.
✓ Develop lists of type and quantity of spaces.
✓ Define specific needs within each space (i.e., number of workstations, storage).
✓ List issues that need clarification or resolution.

Document
✓ Document client's mission and project goals.
✓ Summarize program for current needs and future growth.
✓ Include meeting notes from interviews.
✓ Obtain client approval on program and projections.
✓ Compile detailed report or brief, which is a written document that outlines programmatic goals and all functional, dimensional, and relational requirements.

In 1946, Florence Knoll founded the Planning Unit, an interior design service of H.G. Knoll Associates. Listed as the top two services were analysis of requirements for the project and "preparation of checklists of requirements of the plan with emphasis on flexibility and adaptation to present and future requirements."

hmca Architecture + Design facilitated extensive workshops with the core user group—young children—during the programming phase of their design for the UniverCity Childcare Centre at Simon Frasier University, Burnaby, British Columbia. The resulting space addresses the needs (and heights) of its young occupants.

71 Proportion

The harmonious relationship of parts to each other or to the whole.

See Also
Balance
Form
Ratio
Space

Conceptions of—and attitudes toward—proportion are complicated. What makes something well proportioned? Why are the ratios between some objects considered more pleasing than others? For many, ideas of proportion are complicated by tradition, or by familiarity, but there are a few designated rules that can be useful in thinking through the influence of proportion in design.

The proportion of a space or an object can be described as the relative length of three variables width, length, and height. Proportion in spaces often has a determining role in the function, or use, of that space. A long, narrow corridor cannot be used as a gathering space, but might be ideal for a gallery or a kitchen. A tall, wide space might be too noisy for intimate gatherings, but is ideal for small musical performances. The designer is often presented with a room whose proportions create an opportunity for invention and interpretation, ripe for reimagining based on other principles such as scale and use.

In some interior projects, ideas of proportion and alignment are intimately linked. Even if a room is awkwardly shaped, clever deployment of sectional devices (such as niches, reveals, and recessed elements) can rectify the perceived measurements of the room. Reflective surfaces and patterns can reframe perceptions of space in existing spaces. In any case, the designer should carefully consider the implications of placement, in space or along a wall, of objects in creating an environment crafted to need.

Illustration from Albrecht Dürer's *Vier Bücher von Menschlicher Proportion*, (1528).

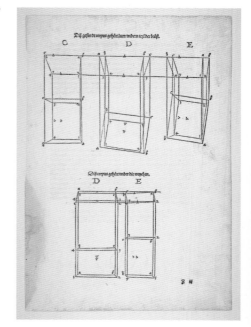

By illuminating the space between the underside of a dropped ceiling and deck above with cove lighting, Merge Architects creates the illusion of height in this meditation space.

High-back chairs and low lighting change the way conversations happen in this lounge space by Muuto.

72 Prototyping

The use of preliminary models and mockups for evaluative purposes.

See Also
Craft
Innovation
Modeling
Technology

The use of prototyping in interior design is similar to how it is used in the other physical design disciplines, such as architecture and industrial engineering. Prototyping takes many forms and is used at various stages of the design process to test out concepts, ideas, and details. Prototypes can be quickly tested in sketches and three-dimensional representations. They are used as a tool to boost creativity and communicate a design idea.

Full-scale mock-ups, 3D printed elements, and larger models are prototyped later in the design process once initial testing has occurred, and are used to test custom elements such as custom wall finishes, cabinet joinery, upholstery, or unique furniture elements. Prototypes can confirm concepts at that key moment prior to full fabrication. Prototyping is iterative by nature; the design evolves by testing it against function, usability, or effect. Mock-ups at this phase are prepared by a fabricator or contractor for designer and client approval.

A study model of a tilt-up pavilion for Boston's Seaport neighborhood by Elle Gerdeman of CO-G.

The firm Hannah explores the potential of large-scale 3D printed concrete for use as structure or furniture.

Small-scale furniture models are part of the design process for Minneapolis-based furniture designer and manufacturer Blu Dot.

73 Ratio

The measurable relationship between two objects or spaces.

See Also
Alignment
Proportion
Rule of Thirds
Volume

Further Reading
John Brownlee, "The Golden Ratio Design's Biggest Myth," *Fast Company*, fastcompany. com/3044877/the-golden-ratio-designs-biggest-myth.

A ratio is the comparison of the size of two or more objects or surfaces relative to each other. This calculation can influence composition, balance, and perceived scale of elements within a space. Closely related to proportion, ratio can be seen as a set of rules that aims to create balance, order, and consistency in a design.

The concept of ratio can be used in the development of a color scheme, where a dominant or base color has a larger presence than other colors. It can be applied to determining the number of chairs that can be placed around a table based on size and comfort, or the adjacency and spacing between sofas and side chairs. High ratios between the size of a surface and elements on it can be utilized to highlight artwork and other objects on a wall; or in the relative sizes between rooms and connecting spaces.

Designers often point to the Golden Ratio as a key metric of a successful composition, but in practice there is no evidence that this ratio is more compelling than other organizing systems, such as the rule of thirds or the rule of a double rectangle. As designers, we are trained to implement organizing systems that are aesthetically pleasing. In practice, however, we should treat these systems as a baseline to help guide decisions about room size and height, placement of furniture in a space, and compositional strategies.

The Golden Ratio has been a standard metric for measuring the success of a composition, but has proven to be arbitrary and easily applied to elements that aren't balanced.

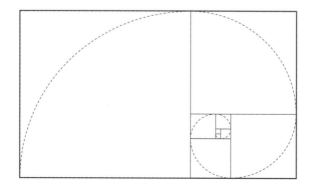

In this room by Arper, the number of chairs, monitors, and elements within a room can affect the proportion and feeling of a room.

The colors of the large-scale ottomans by Muuto are used proportionally to the wall covering and matte black wall.

74 Red Thread

The feature, theme, or element that ties together a space or multiple spaces.

See Also
Color Scheme
Furniture
Placement
Storytelling

The golden thread (originally referred to as the "red thread" in Swedish and Nordic culture) is a concept or feature that exists in every part of something, binding it together and giving it value. It comes from the Greek myth of Theseus and the Minotaur, in which Theseus found his way out of the trap of the Minotaur's labyrinth by following the red thread he was given by Ariadne.

In an interior, the idea of the red thread is manifest through the recurrence of materials, colors, or other artifacts in a design. While it's certainly not possible or necessary to use a physical thread to tie together a space, the repetition of like elements can lead to a more unified design overall. These repeated core elements add strength and cohesion to a project that could be seen as disjointed (whether through spatial conditions or eclectic clashes of material) and can cue recognition of these elements from one room to another.

There are several ways in which a conceptual thread can be used to tie together a design

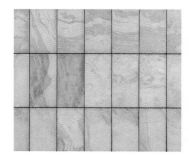

Color
Selecting a base color for each space (typically a neutral white) or introduces a subtle tone that functions as a background for the addition of furniture and other elements.

Material
Using consistent touch, weave, and placement of the various materials used in the space.

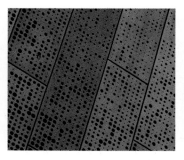

Detailing
Including details that are repeated in common design elements (door frames, counters), or that show how the connections of surfaces are resolved. This can occasionally be changed if an element needs emphasis.

Theme
Choosing an approach that aggregates from room to room. Often the art in a space is an element that can be used to support a theme. Teasing out themes and patterns in the selection and placement of art, and using similar mounting heights and framing types can bring consistency to a space.

From electric cords to furniture legs to detailing on custom millwork, the color orange is the red thread in this maker space at the Park School in Brookline, Massachusetts, designed by Utile.

Various shades of blue—in floor coverings, in furnishings, and a graphic Baux Acoustic Tile wall—contribute to a common palette in this office lounge in KMPG's headquarters in Copenhagen designed by Francisco Sarria.

75 Regionalism

The design features that are particular to a culture's tradition and history.

See Also
Character
Detail
History
Philosophy

Regionalism is the close examination of history and progress through the lens of a designer's immediate geographic, cultural, and social context. It has a complex and contentious history within the design profession, as it has been perceived as an attempt to move away from a design culture that emphasizes innovation and progress.

The main theory of a regionalist approach came as a response to both the perceived monolithic aesthetics of the modern movement and the subsequent shift to historical reference in the postmodern period. The architectural historian Kenneth Frampton posited a theory toward a critical regionalism in an eponymous essay in 1983 "Critical regionalism should adopt modern architecture, critically, for its universal progressive qualities but at the same time value should be placed on the geographical context of the building."

Regionalist design solutions look to their immediate environment, vernacular traditions, and materials choices that resonate with the designer and the users of the space. The resultant designs are considered to be more sympathetic with their surroundings, use form and materials in ways that align with a locale, and attempt to mediate between the forces of globalization, while not preventing modern design.

The interior of Utzon's Sydney Opera House.

The interior of the Bagsværd Church designed by Jørn Utzon in Copenhagen, Denmark. The vaults and soft light echo traditional ecclesiastical design, while retaining a modern sensibility.

In this residence, the Egyptian architect Hassan Fathy used ancient forms updated with contemporary construction techniques to develop a highly regional aesthetic.

76 Representation

The use of drawings and diagrams to explain a design.

See Also
Composition
Design Process
Modeling
Perspective

Resources

marcusperspective. com marker-based representations that are full of life and vitality.

www.youtube.com/c/ LearnUpstairs features easily accessible web-based tutorials that focus on digital techniques that enhance and facilitate image-making.

Representation is the most important communication tool that an interior designer has. The representation of a project can enhance the ideas about design intent, facilitate decisions about spatial ideas and materials, and through objective drawing methods describe aspects of a project that otherwise cannot be visualized. Representation is much more than a drawing that describes the design of a project; it embodies the intent of a project, and can be much more interpretive and subjective, showing the user's point of view. In essence, representation is a visual narrative that explains the intent of the design concept.

There are many online communities and online tutorials that can help explain the function of representation in design, as well as both the software used and the skills and techniques that a designer needs to develop. These range from the creation of photo-realistic imagery, to other representations that use drawing conventions to explain the features integral to a design. These drawings use transparent and exploded diagramming techniques to explain a project to an audience.

In addition to renderings and delineated drawings, the designer should consider using illustrations that are more abstract, such as collages, materials compositions, or hand diagrams and sketches, all of which can represent the mood and the impressions of a design project.

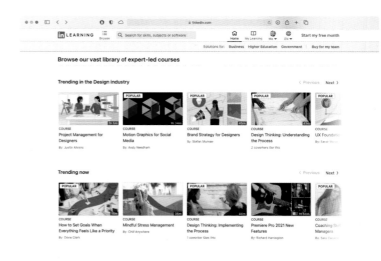

Hand sketches by Houston designer and lecturer Marcus Martinez render design solutions with whim and vitality.

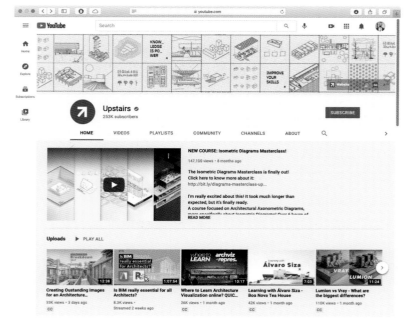

Video-based instruction has opened up access to sources of continuing education for interior designers. Sites such as YouTube's "Upstairs" and LinkedIn's "Learning" (formerly Lynda.com), offer paid content, but can be accessed with a library card.

77 Rhythm

The movement, fluctuation, or variation marked by the regular recurrence or flow of related design elements.

See Also
Grid
Measurement
Movement
Texture

Rhythm plays a significant role in the development of an interior. When design elements are repeated, the intervals between those repetitions establish a sense of rhythm and movement to create visual interest. Elements of rhythm allow patterns to flow with progression, transition, and repetitions. Similar colors, materials, shapes, or gradations of elements from small to large contribute to this impression of movement as one experiences the space.

There are three types of rhythm in interior design

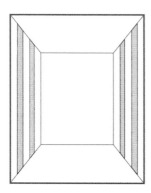

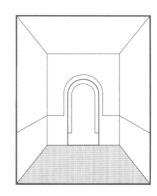

Repetition
Repeating design elements throughout a space. Examples include textiles, patterning, colors, textures, line, light, or objects. Designers are able to create a flow through space by repeating these elements.

Progression
Also called *gradation*, progression in rhythm is created with continuity and can work with various shapes, sizes, and colors. For example, rhythm can be achieved by arranging objects in sizes progressing from small to large, as in nesting tables or storage bins. Gradating light and color (as in transitioning from dark to light in shades or tones), is another example of progression. All of these gradual increases in size, light, shape, or color can add a sense of depth and movement to a space.

Transition
Transitional rhythm is implemented visually with a continuous flow across a space or along the path of travel. This type of rhythm is often an architectural feature or furniture piece, such as stair rails, dining tables, arches, or windows that offer scenic views. With transitional rhythm, the eye follows a line from one point in the room to another, guided by strategically incorporated design elements.

Universal Principles of Interior Design

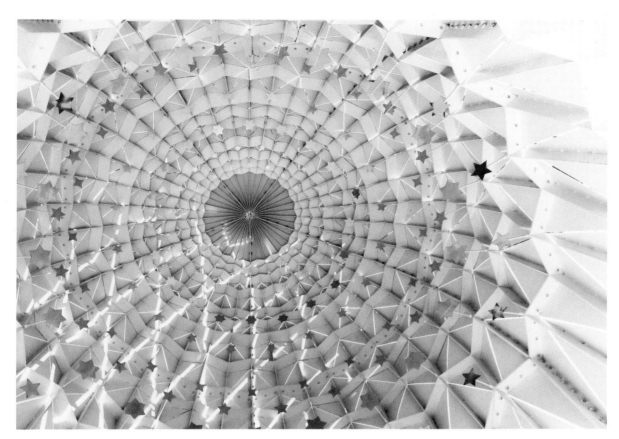

The repetitive and rhythmic interior of *Khalvat* (2014), a scupture by the Iranian artist Sahand Hesamiyan.

Different scales become a playground of Button Ottomans by Kelly Harris Smith.

78 Rule of Thirds

A compositional system that gives structure to an image or space.

See Also
Balance
Hierarchy
Perspective
Representation

The rule of thirds is a system, originally from fine art painting, that divides a composition into a nine-square grid. The rule discourages the placement of the main subject of an image at the visual center of a frame, and prefers placement along one of the axes instead.

While this rule is framed around a static point of view, it can be useful in determining how to place objects when seen through the various apertures and framing devices that designers use—doors, windows, and larger openings. In addition, stand-alone elements that horizontally divide a space, such as a counter, shelf, or table can be used to enhance one of the main axes.

When composing wall elevations, the rule of thirds can help direct the placement of artwork, suggest locations for wall lighting, and indicate where breaks in material, reveals, and changes in finish or color may occur.

It is also a good compositional rule to consider when taking the final photos of a project. Take a cue from professional photographers and turn on a rule of thirds grid overlay on your camera while looking for scouting shots to help determine what images are important to the project.

In composing a space or an image, the internal intersections (circled below) provide axes' for horizontal and vertical alignment with objects of interest. These grids are easily enabled in digital photography and 3D applications.

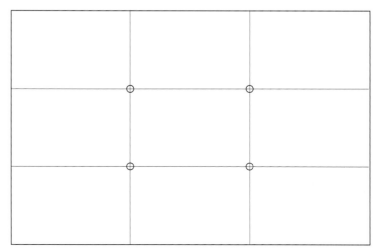

A rule of thirds grid overlaid on a photograph. Critical alignments are made to ensure that proportion and point of view are balanced in the frame.

A nook for a desk uses desk elements, shelves, and hanging light fixtures to determine proper rule of thirds placement.

79 Scale

The series of marks or points that measure distances;
the proportion between two sets of dimensions.

See Also Depth
Form
Proportion
Ratio

Scale has a number of meanings within the discipline of interior design. It can refer to a method of delineation in technical drawing, the measure of distance in space, or the system of proportion that relates the size of objects to each other.

The idea of a scaled drawing has existed for centuries, as evidenced in some of Leonardo da Vinci's earliest drawings. The idea of scaled drawings communicating design can be found in aincent delineations, but was formalized during the Industrial Revolution, when notational systems were deployed to represent the idea of the full-sized object in delineated form. These are typically related as the proportion of a measurable line to its full-size equivalent; for instance, $1/8" = 1'\text{-}0"$, or 1100. Each scale has a specific purpose in the communication of a design project. Types of scaled drawings include plans, sections, orthographic projections or any drawing that can be measured.

The other, less didactic, reference to scale in interior design refers to proportion; more specifically, it relates to the relative size of one object to another in a volume or on a surface. A large object in a smaller room will overwhelm the space and be considered out of scale, while a small object in a taller space will look equally out of place. The reliance on harmonious systems of balance, such as ratio and proportion, should not be overlooked. Ideas of "correct" sizing are always up for interpretation or radical reimagining.

Scale		Use
Imperial System of Measurement	International System of Units (SI)	
1/32" and above	1500 and above	Site and urban drawings
1/16"	1200	Overall plan drawing
1/4"	1100	Enlarged plans, sections, and millwork drawings
1/2"	110	Details and enlarged section drawings
Full Scale	11	Highly specific connections

Various drawing types have their own communicative use. The smaller the ratio between measurements, the more information a drawing can convey. A millwork detail sheet begins to describe the fabrication of two built-in elements.

The repetition of elements and small artwork make the Patricia Ready Art Gallery, by elton_léniz and Izquierdo Lehmann in Santiago, Chile, appear vast.

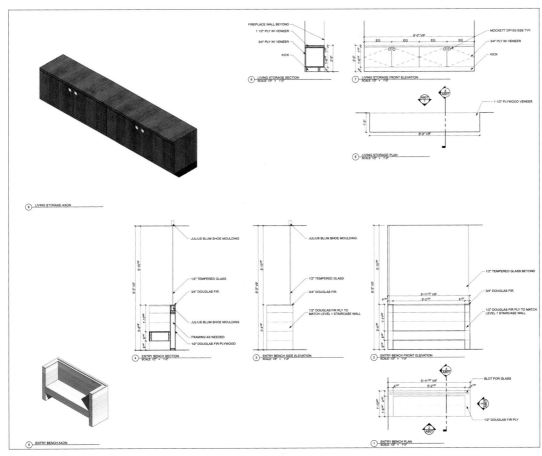

80 Shape

A two-dimensional area defined by the outline of an object.

See Also
Form
Geometry
Organic
Volume

Natural or organic shapes are those that are inspired by or are found in nature—leaves, flora, clouds, rivers and ocean waves, and landscapes. Objects that are inspired by nature, or include nature itself, provide a softness and calming feel in a space.

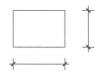

Geometric shapes are mathematically defined, and contain measured areas and sizes. These elements are made from the base geometry of squares, triangles, rectangles, circles, and various "-gons" and "-grams."

Abstract shapes, sometimes referred to as "non-objective" or "blobs," are created by artists or designers using random lines and edges. They may be variations or combinations of geometric or natural shapes, but are designed with an intentional eye toward function and use.

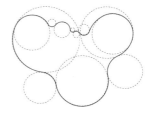

Curved shapes move the eye, and are often softer and more approachable, while shapes with sharp angles and edges depict strength and symbolize structure and order.

Shape can be explored in an interior as a three-dimensional strategy. By careful examination of the architecture and volume of the space, the placement or arrangement of furniture can shape the perception of how it is to be used. Through the actual contours of furniture, lighting, and elements in a space, shapes bring focus and attention to a particular object or shape through two-dimensional patterning on textiles, wall tiles, flooring, or drapery.

A ginkgo leaf, measured forms, and the described arcs of Alvar Aalto's vase, designed in 1937.

Cloud & Co. gelato shop in Doha takes inspiration from M.C. Escher's whimsical geometric artwork with bold shapes in the form of architectural built-ins and decor.

A school in Billund, Denmark, uses playful shapes to create an active, curving landscape.

81 Sight Lines

The unobstructed view extending from a viewer to an object, space, or landscape beyond.

See Also
Emphasis
Perspective
Wayfinding

Helpful Advice
Strategic placement of mirrors in a home (or in other spaces) can reflect a view and contribute to expansive site lines through a space.

Sight lines are an important consideration in interior design. Loosely defined as the implied line connecting the viewer and the subject of their interest, sight lines function as an active tool for navigation and comprehension of a space.

Sight lines are a vital part of the planning process for the design of civic structures, such as auditoriums, stadiums, or theaters. They aid in determining the configuration of seating and allow spectators to see all areas of a playing field or theater stage; sight lines also provide visual access for passive safety and security. An important consideration in this type of project is that of the "C-value," which is defined as the vertical distance from the viewer's eyes to the sight line of the viewer directly behind, which ultimately defines the rake, or upward slope of the seating.

In many projects, the idea of a view corridor—a line of sight between an active observer and their final destination or object located at a distance—is critical for implied movement within a space. Sight lines are useful in wayfinding by providing clear landmarks within a design, and give the navigator a more expansive view to move in a particular direction. In an exhibition or museum context, sight lines provide information about what's ahead to complement and enhance the narratives of exhibit or display.

In a residence, visual connections from one space to another can enhance flow, and provide a sense of openness and accessibility. Creating broad sight lines from kitchen spaces into living areas and dining rooms is a common planning tactic in residential design. Double-height spaces or clerestory windows increase vertical sight lines and allow more light. Private spaces, such as bedrooms and bathrooms, do not require the same level of accessibility.

Sight lines are critical in the interior environment of a hospital. In the Penn State Health Milton S. Hershey Medical Center by Payette, open spaces, light, and clear graphics provide easy visual access to services.

The Oslo Public Library, designed by Lund Hagem Arkitekter AS, uses double-height spaces, views through to other floors as a of enabling navigation.

82 Social Impact

The use of design strategies and tactical solutions to bring about positive social change.

See Also
Accessibility
Adaptability
Human-Centered
  Design
Inclusivity

References
*Jennifer Rittner, "What Is Design for Social Impact?," School of Visual Arts, New York, productsofdesign.sva.edu/blog/what-is-design-for-social-impact.

**HMCA, "Designing for Inclusivity," hcma.ca/tilt/open-assets/.

Designing for social impact is the "practice of interrogating systems—institutional, economic, social, political, interpersonal—in order to define opportunities for change that give voice to those who have been disenfranchised or marginalized by design."*

This is a relatively new field of study that has emerged over the last thirty years. It is not limited to interior design, but exists as a strategy across multiple design disciplines, including product design, graphic design, architecture, landscape design, and interiors. This effort uses the existing tools of the design process to examine biases, eliminate and reduce power imbalances, and address the implications of harmful stereotypes in a design.

Any process of change requires that we work in collaborative environments, reassess our role in design decisions, and challenge ourselves to design with and in response to addressing who our collaborators are. This is a difficult and ultimately messy process; while there are short-term successes, failures should also be part of the work. Extensive assessment, observation, and feedback over the long term will enable the results to be more effective.

To serve the diverse needs of the community, MKCA designed the Children's Library at Concourse House in the Bronx, New York and provided all design and architecture services pro-bono. In addition, they solicited in-kind donations from designers, suppliers, fabricators, and contractors to help complete the project.

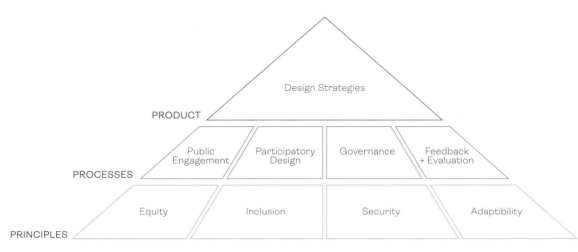

Design Strategies

PRODUCT

Public Engagement | Participatory Design | Governance | Feedback + Evaluation

PROCESSES

Equity | Inclusion | Security | Adaptibility

PRINCIPLES

Social Impact Framework Diagram was created by HCMA** to "help fill a gap in design knowledge around issues relating to universal washrooms and change rooms, and their provision in community and recreation facilities."

83 Space

The dimension of a surface or volume.

See Also
Composition
Function
Proportion
Volume

In interior design, there are two types of space two-dimensional and three-dimensional. The space of a project is the base canvas on which a designer begins to develop a project. It is by measuring—the area of an element in a project (the two-dimensional length and width of a floor or wall that determines quantities of materials) and the volume of a room (the three-dimensional height that is used for calculations of air flow and circulation, light levels, and structural needs).

Space is also referred to as "positive space" or "negative space." Positive space contains objects—furniture, fixtures, artwork, and other styling elements, while negative space is the "empty" part of the volume or surface that you are designing. The balance between positive and negative space is an important aspect of the composition of and navigation through a space. If there are too many objects in a room (too much positive space), the resulting design can appear cluttered or visually noisy. This can be used as a design strategy—think of a den, a portrait gallery, or a library where aggregation is part of a collection or curatorial intent. Conversely, a large volume of space containing fewer elements has a sense of calm, and can emphasize the objects in the space (which is a typical minimalist design approach). Open spaces, such as spas and modern museum galleries or residences with an abundance of room, are more successful where light is plentiful.

Often the space of an interior is determined by the existing conditions of a project. The designer can direct decisions about openings in both horizontal and vertical directions with a structural engineer, to access physical and visual connections within a project. Existing structural limitations will influence the intended use of an interior, the number of elements that can be placed within it, and how color and textures affect the perceptions of a surface or volume.

In Diller Scofidio + Renfro's design for the Broad, an art museum in Los Angeles, the negative space of the gallery is used to improve sight lines, while the more active facade design filters light through a series of positive space apertures.

See Also

Environmental psychology is a branch of psychology that explores the relationship between humans and the external world.

Organizations include the Project for Public Spaces, the Center for Human Environments in New York, and the International Association of People-Environment Studies.

A double-height volume at the Linnaeus Library in Småland brings light deep into the space, and allows visual access to the collection.

In the Large Italian Skylight Hall at the Hermitage Museum in St. Petersburg, Russia, the aggregation of paintings hanging on vibrant walls offers an active viewing pattern.

84 Specifications

The method of describing design intent and furnishings.

See Also
Acoustics
Codes
Health, Safety,
  and Welfare
Materiality

Further Reading
Lisa Godsey, *Interior
Design Materials and
Specifications* (Fairchild
Books, 2017).

Specifications are written documents that detail all the elements and expected levels of craft and published standards of a project. They contain textual descriptions of all elements of a project—such as finish types, lighting, substrates, and furniture. They are used (alongside design drawings, schedules, and design details) to solicit competitive bids from contractors and suppliers.

There are two categories of specification documents open and closed, which are sometimes referred to as "prescriptive" or "proprietary." Open (prescriptive) specifications are developed around performance, and allow for substitutions and competitive bids. Closed (proprietary) specifications are for elements that must be in a project, which names a specific element (such as a piece of furniture from a single manufacturer) and limits acceptable substitutions. Each specification category is connected to the type of project; for instance, commercial projects are best served by open specification because they are more general in scope with more flexibility for acceptable substitutes and options. The more specific a project (such as a high-end retail space with corporate standards, or a residential project with a client who requires exact finishes for a finished product) requires a closed spec.

In addition, the language and syntax contained within specification documents are highly formalized. In North America, two formats dominate MasterSpec and MasterFormat. There are specialized consultants and softwares that are used for specification writing, so the type of project should be taken into consideration before deciding on which specifications are appropriate.

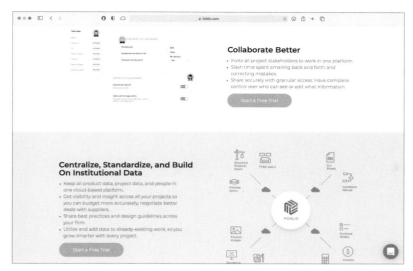

Collaborate Better

- Invite all project stakeholders to work in one platform.
- Slash time spent emailing back and forth and correcting mistakes.
- Share securely with granular access: Have complete control over who can see or edit what information.

Start a Free Trial

Centralize, Standardize, and Build On Institutional Data

- Keep all product data, project data, and people in one cloud-based platform.
- Get visibility and insight across all your projects so you can budget more accurately, negotiate better deals with suppliers.
- Share best practices and design guidelines across your firm.
- Utilize and add data to already-existing work, so you grow smarter with every project.

Start a Free Trial

Specification software, such as fohlio.com, cut sheets from furniture companies, and close attention to material and furniture submittals will ensure that the specified product is installed with accuracy.

KURVE COLLECTION

DESIGN BY ALAN DANDRON & AVERY HANDY

LOUNGE SELECTIONS

Chair 480-04
Low Back
Width: 30"
Depth: 30"
Height: 33"
Seat Height: 17"
Arm Height: 23.5"

Chair 480-01
Swivel
Width: 33"
Depth: 34"
Height: 39.5"
Seat Height: 17"
Arm Height: 24.5"

Chair 480-03
Swivel Wing
Width: 33"
Depth: 34"
Height: 39.5"
Seat Height: 17"
Arm Height: 24.5"

Ottoman 480-02
Width: 24"
Depth: 24"
Height: 16.5"

Bench 480-50B
Width: 50"
Depth: 24"
Height: 16.5"

TABLE SELECTIONS

Table 481-24CL
Width: 24"
Depth: 24"
Height: 16"

Table 481-24CH
Width: 24"
Depth: 24"
Height: 20"

Table 481-20CH
Width: 20"
Depth: 20"
Height: 20"

Table 481-24SL
Width: 24"
Depth: 24"
Height: 16"

Table 481-20SH
Width: 20"
Depth: 20"
Height: 20"

Refer to martinbrattrud.com for complete style specifications, options and pricing.

Martin Brattrud   1224 West 132nd Street Gardena, California 90247   tel 323 770 4171   fax 323 770 4503   martinbrattrud.com

85 Storytelling

Relating a narrative about, by, or for a user's relationship to a space.

See Also
Character
Mood
Regionalism
Styling

Storytelling in interior design is the creation of a narrative or journey, of an environment through careful space and object planning. It is a helpful tool in developing and determining choices about colors, palettes, materials, and furniture, and can be applied to residential, commercial, and other types of interior spaces. Storytelling is exceptionally useful in spaces where narratives drive an experience, such as museum exhibits and retail environments.

Narratives help foster an emotional connection between the design and the user interacting with the design. By communicating information in a visual way, the designer establishes a connection with the users of a space.

Prior to the development of written language, humans communicated their histories by telling stories and drawing pictures. In the process, these stories intimately tied these histories to memory, with many early orators using an imagined space—a method of *loci*, or memory palace—as a mnemonic device. This imagined physical space held objects that tied together collective memories. Aristotle, in his framework for rhetoric, described seven essential components of a narrative—plot, character, theme, diction, melody, decor, and spectacle. Not all listed are relevant to interior design, but several can be helpful as techniques to gain insight into users, build empathy, and connect emotionally through design.

The role of space in our collective memory is explored in Frances Yates's *The Art of Memory*, which looks at the mnemonic methods of early storytellers, such as those described by Cicero in his treatise, "De Oratore."

Jill Malek designed this custom wallcovering inspired by traditional Chinese landscape painting for the upscale Chinese restaurant Red Plate, in Las Vegas, Nevada, in collaboration with Celano Design Studio.

Sonnhild Kestler's colorful wallcovering for Maharam Digital projects, called "Arche Noah," is "composed of dozens of individual silk-screened shapes, arranged to form motifs that range from the playfully abstract to the discernibly representational."

86 Styling

The way in which something is intentionally positioned within a space for visual interest.

See Also
Character
Layering
Mood
Storytelling

Further Reading
Frida Ramstedt,
*The Interior Design
Handbook Furnish,
Decorate, and Style Your
Space* (Clarkson Potter,
2020).

Emily Henderson, *Styled
Secrets for Arranging
Rooms, from Tabletops
to Bookshelves* (Potter
Style, 2015).

Styling is the use of objects—books, artwork, sculpture, or plants—to achieve compositional balance and add detail to what is otherwise a blank moment in a design. The positioning of furniture, placement of accessories, and the addition of wall and flooring choices all contribute to the successful documentation of a project.

Styling within a space can also have a functional component, and is accomplished through the intentional placement of a mixture of accessories, smaller decorative elements, artwork, and the furniture on which items are displayed.

Accessories used for styling are smaller than furniture and contribute to the visual field of an interior. These functional accessories include vases or planters, a magazine stand, wall clocks, or sentimental items like framed photographs or souvenirs. These elements are deemed worthy of display rather than stored away unseen.

In addition, the introduction of smaller-scale elements within an overall design provides insight into the person, family, or company who use the space daily.

The aggregation of artwork, vegetation, books, and art objects establishes tone and character, and provides visual interest in this interior by Jessica Klein.

Still-life styling consists of intentionally formed groupings that reinforce a style or mood. These collections are often more dynamic when the grouped elements vary in size, height, shape, color, or texture.

87 Surface

The outermost layer of the objects and materials in a space.

See Also
Craft
Finishes
Materiality
Texture

Surface is the final layer of a project, and like many other principles of interior design, it has resonance with the aural, visual, and tactile qualities of a design.

Surfaces are the main experience of an interior—paint on walls, flooring, laminates on cabinetry, fabrics on furnishings. Surfaces are closely aligned with acoustics; they have reflective and absorptive qualities that add to the aural perception of a project. Color, whether integral to material or applied, also reflects or absorbs the light in a room. Texture—subtle surface deformations, stitching in fabric, or the smooth finish of a plaster wall—allows for the touch and feel of objects and surfaces.

There are essentially two types of surfaces in the physical world diffuse and metallic. Diffuse materials have a roughness to them that sends light rays scattering in all directions, which makes an object appear to have varying levels of roughness. This effect, known as the "Fresnel effect," states that the amount of light reflected from a surface depends on the viewing angle at which it is perceived. Metallic surfaces are defined by their periodic table of elements—gold, silver, copper, aluminum, or iron. They are good conductors of heat and electricity. In addition, metallic surfaces have absorptive, specular, and refractive qualities that should be taken into consideration.

Of all the tools that interior designers use to define space, surfaces are perhaps the simplest and, at the same time, most complex. The impact of the detailed, behind-the-scenes work that allows an interior to function effectively will be lost unless the finished surfaces are well integrated into the project.

In Detroit's Fisher Building (1928), one of the most impressive commercial interiors desginced by Albert Kahn, the art deco interiors gleam with opulent surfaces.

The multicolored surfaces are focus elements in this coworking office by Ivy Studio in Montréal, Canada.

This Kyiv, Ukraine, restaurant designed by Yakusha Design uses multiple scales and articulations of surface to welcome customers to the space.

88 Sustainability

A method of harvesting or using a resource so that it is not depleted.

See Also
Biophilia
Circular Design
Durability
Natural Lighting

The main considerations when designing a sustainable interior should be to mitigate the effects of climate change, reduce waste, and encourage the reuse and recyclability of materials. Designers should be aware of several factors that encourage the use of sustainable materials and products.

Certifying Agencies
UL Certified
Green Building Challenge
The Lacey Act
Health Product
Declarations
Forest Stewardship
Council (FSC)
Cradle to Cradle
Intertek

Life Cycle Assessment
Declare
Level
U.S. Green Building
Council
Healthier Hospitals
Mindful Materials
Living Building Challenge
Well Building Institute

Healthy Environments

Spaces that can maintain improved air quality, efficient heating, natural ventilation, and correct acoustics, and promote healthier occupancy. This can be achieved by the use of low volatile organic compounds (VOC) emissions or toxins from furniture or products, and incorporating plants to offset carbon dioxide.

Energy Efficiency

Aims to reduce the amount of energy needed for heating, lighting, and appliances. From a product selection standpoint, this includes using energy-efficient lighting, as well as interior and exterior window treatments to offset natural heat gain, or conversely to take advantage of sunlight and solar panels. Ensuring proper insulation, floor assemblies, radiant flooring, and carpets provides thermal insulators at a building's perimeter.

Waste Reduction

By recycling, upcycling, and repurposing materials, designers can reduce waste. Opting for synthetic materials that are made from recycled materials can also minimize and divert waste from landfills. In the cradle-to-cradle approach, waste material becomes new products, forming a circular loop.

Longevity and Flexibility

When selecting durable materials, choose quality over quantity. Life cycle assessment (LCA) is a methodology that evaluates the entire life cycle of a product, including extraction, production, transportation, processing, and waste disposal or recovery of materials.

Lower Environmental Impact

Choose materials with the lowest impact on the environment, such as wood, wool, and stone, and highly renewable materials like bamboo or cork. There are many third-party certifications, initiatives, and rating systems that exist in most countries that rank or reward projects or products with wellness declarations.

Arper's seating collection Mixu was designed in collaboration with Gensler with two goals in mind—designer customization and sustainability. Designed for disassembly, Mixu offers designers the ability to mix and match post-industrial recycled plastics, FSC certified woods, recycled steel and an infinite number of upholstery options all without any adhesives, staples or comolded materials.

Interface is a leading sustainable flooring manufacturer, using 99 percent renewable energy and a minimum of 66 to 80 percent recycled content in their flooring products. It also publishes all ingredients in Health Product Declarations (HPDs). Each product has an Environmental Product Declaration (EPD) that evaluates factors based on full life cycle assessment (LCA).

89 Symbolism

The attribution of meaning to objects and spaces.

See Also
Color Palette
Mood
Space
Tone

Symbols, or iconic elements, have a performative role by presenting objects that suggest the use of a space. Symbols are iconic—if you ask a child to draw a house, they immediately draw a box topped with a triangle to imply dwelling. Symbols are a learned and acquired visual language that has cultural and historical connections to spaces. The most obvious use of symbolism in an interior is in civic and religious spaces; the gravitas of a city seal over a door, or the minbar of a mosque, suggests the authority or reverence that these places elicit.

Symbolism can also be implemented in less formal and unexpected ways a large framed opening in a room can be symbolic of direction or suggest performance; or the shape of a window can symbolize its function and type. In older office layouts, the large corner office symbolized leadership and power, which in today's office landscape has been replaced by open space and horizontal structures. Gatherings of couches and soft seating suggest a less top-heavy hierarchy and more relaxed attitude toward work.

Color can also be a symbol of mood and tone, and varies according to culture and tradition. Bold colors with intense hues symbolize energy and optimism, while natural tones indicate calm, quiet, or contemplation.

In the prayer hall at the Cambridge Central Mosque by Marks Barfield Architects, timber columns rise to skylit openings that speak of connection to a higher being.

In a similar way, the lily pad columns inside the Great Workroom in Frank Lloyd Wright's Johnson Wax headquarters in Racine, Wisconsin, provide implied protection and wonder for the workers below.

The dramatic use of stauary, *bas-relief*, and ornate detailing in the Justizpalast in Vienna, Austria command authority and reverence.

90 Symmetry

The effect when elements are reflected on opposite sides of an axis or center point.

See Also
Asymmetry
Composition
Line
Placement

In traditional interior layouts and spaces, the use of symmetry is often the basis for the development of the placement of elements and furniture. It is also closely related to the principle of balance, which aims for an equal distribution of objects in a room or volume.

Establishing a strong axis as the dominant feature in a space—such as an element of furniture, flooring, or a ceiling fixture—creates the center line through which objects are mirrored. Smaller rooms benefit from symmetrical layouts, as the requirements for circulation often dictate the need for a legible arrangement. Spaces such as dining rooms and bedrooms in residential design, and meeting rooms and classrooms in commercial and academic design often require symmetrical solutions.

Radial symmetry focuses arrangement around a single point. Spaces that are in the round, or have enough space for circulation can benefit from this approach. In this type of symmetry, ceiling fixtures or sculptural artwork can become organizing elements.

Symmetrical staircases encircle the drum-shaped Reading Room and its glazed canopy at the center of the Great Court in the British Museum by Foster + Partners.

Two long benches and chairs designed by Lievore Altherr Molina for Arper bracket this linear mirroring of elements.

The conversation pit at the Miller house in Columbus, Indiana, designed by Eero Saarinen & Associates (1957), uses localized symmetry to define space. The area is offset in the overall plan, but organizes the surrounding elements.

91 Technology

The use of computational devices to aid design and enhance space.

See Also
Acoustics
Modeling
Modularity
Perspective

Further Reading
Megan Schellong, "How Virtual Reality Is Used To Help Recognize Unconsciou Biases,"
www.npr.org/ 2021/05/19/998137110/ how-virtual-reali-ty-is-used-to-help-recog-nize-unconscious-biases.

Technology is increasingly becoming integrated into our built environment, as more connected devices aid in the function of programmed items and spaces. Apps, connected devices, and smart speakers allow for control over elements in a home (locks, lights, temperature controls), provide accessible options to create and maintain sustainable lighting and environmental control, and make the use of space easier through voice control. In commercial and retail spaces, the integration of touch screens for wayfinding, identifying room schedule and use, testing choices through virtual fitting rooms, and transforming the way we navigate cultural spaces allow for deeper experiences and equitable solutions.

Technology is also a dominant factor in the choice and implementation of design tools. It is increasingly used for integrated project delivery, communication between clients and contractors, augmented and virtual reality for supporting design decisions, and recognition of biases. The advancement and sophistication of on-demand printing for fabrication of custom pieces demonstrate the ubiquity of technology in the profession.

However, overreliance on technology is not without a caveat—the pace of technological advances often makes even the latest generation of a device or integrated technologies redundant. Companies are acquired and abandoned. Cutting-edge solutions are often expensive and require maintenance. Also, issues of privacy should be considered carefully when specifying connected devices for a project.

Joris Laarman Lab embraces novel digital fabrication methods, including robotic welding.

The kinetic sculpture
"Diffusion Choir" by
SoSo Limited animates
this lobby in Cambridge,
Massachusetts,
by simulating the
movements of an
invisible flock of birds.

SOM's Mumbai International Airport is composed
of several complex columns that simultaneously
allow light and provide structure.

92 Texture

The visual or tactile surface characteristics and appearance of a material.

See Also
Craft
Detail
Finishes
Surface

Further Reading
Fashionary, *Textilepedia* (Fashionary International Limited, 2020).

Kelly Wearstler, *Evocative Style* (Rizzoli, 2019).

There are two basic types of texture in interior design visual and tactile. Examples of materials with visual texture are wood and stone, typically smooth to touch, and defined by their natural grain and veining. Tactile textures have a three-dimensional quality that can be felt with one's hand and include textiles or carpets, which may be hand- or machine-crafted, and can vary from smooth to rough or uneven, but add to the overall character of a space.

To work with texture, interior designers must consider the effects of shadow and reflection caused by the surface configuration of materials, including textiles, stone, wood, glass, metals, and painted walls. Many materials respond differently in varying lighting, natural or artificial; therefore, integration of these textures requires a careful combination of lighting design with material selection.

Textures are most effectively utilized when they are strategically positioned adjacent to a contrasting texture, such as a rough texture next to a smooth texture, a matte surface next to a reflective surface, or an opaque material near a translucent material. The interaction of color, material, and texture, and how they are affected by lighting all contribute to the character of the interior environment.

Examples of material textures frosted glass, recycled cotton and cork rug by Kelly Harris Smith for SUGO, and board-formed concrete.

Jessica Klein's design for a Boston, Massachusetts residence incorporates multiple visual and tactile textures within an earth-toned color palette.

The set at Mercedes-Benz Fashion Week Australia in Sydney incorporates myriad visual and tactile textures, all within a neutral palette.

93 Tone

The character or quality of a space.

See Also
Character
Finishes
Gradation
Materiality

Designers use tone to create a dominant mood in a space, which is also related to a project's color scheme. Tone can also aid in developing the character of a project, and influencing the psychology of the inhabitants of the space. In color theory terms, tone is defined as the mix of tint (white) and shade (black), and is understood as the lightness or brightness of a color.

Tone can be utilized to alter the proportions of a space, and its effects vary depending on intensity. The deeper the tone, the more light absorbed. This has the effect of the color appearing closer to the viewer, and the room appearing heavier. Lighter tones reflect more light, and as a result, the color often appears further away, making the room appear airier and spacious.

Designers often establish the mood of their projects with the inclusion of the following tonal groupings

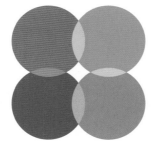

Warm Tones
Oranges, yellows, and reds.

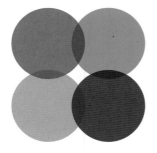

Cool Tones
Blues, greens and purples.

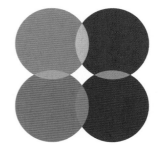

Earth Tones
Oranges, reds, blues, and browns.

Jewel Tones
Pastels, light blues, and turquoises.

Merge Architects utilized tonal colors in the selection of materials to distinguish three otherwise identical conference rooms of a tech workplace in Cambridge, Massachusetts.

Still Life (1943) by Italian painter Giorgio Morandi. Morandi is known for his still life paintings with their tonal subtlety in depicting simple subjects/objects.

Our perception of how light or dark something may be is influenced by the field in which it is placed. The same fifty-percent grey surrounded by black and white plays a trick on the eyes. Because of different tonal backgrounds, one dot appears much darker than the other.

93 Tone

94 Transparency

The quality and quantity of light that passes through an object.

See Also
Apertures
Finishes
Layering
Natural Lighting

The spectrum between transparency and opacity offers a range of opportunities for the designer. Based on their role and function in an interior, transparent elements do not have to provide visual access or operability, but they still have functional purposes. Interior windows, partitions, and mirrors can offer strategic views into other spaces, obscure vision at key moments for privacy when needed (while still allowing access to light and views), and enlarge a room through reflection. Translucent surfaces can also have the illusion of depth, either through surface effects, or by backlighting or back painting.

Translucency The transmission and diffusion of light so that objects beyond cannot be clearly seen.

Opacity The quality, light transmission, or state of an object that makes it impervious to light.

Types of Transparent Surfaces/Materials	
Hard Surfaces	Glass, Acrylic, Plastic, Fiberglass
Soft Surfaces	Scrims, Screens, Textiles

Transparent   Translucent   Opaque

A glass screen by Ronan and Erwan Bouroullec for Skyline Design provides visual privacy in this meeting area.

In the HE Art Museum in Guangdong, China, by Tadao Ando, an architectural screen is designed to divide space while maintaining visual access.

A translucent screen divides this office space while still allowing light to pass through.

95 Typology

A classification system that categorizes and describes different types of design.

See Also
Function
Hybridization
Program
Regionalism

Interior design is a varied, robust, and diverse profession. Interior designers work across multiple markets, and many design offices or solo practitioners operate in many different types of studios, out of necessity and expertise—from large corporate offices to small practices.

Deciding which aspect of interior design to pursue comes down to experience—there are similar needs and processes of each type of interior design that overlap, both in technical requirements and programming needs that make it easy for a young designer to sample the different kinds of work environments of the profession. In addition, the strict isolation of disciplinary practices has eroded in recent years. For instance, there is an increasing use of residential typologies in commercial offices (living rooms), and the sudden need to work from home has brought external needs into the home in an unprecedented way.

Some of the many typologies of interior design practice are outlined below. Each have their own fee structures and levels of expertise. The common thread of all is a commitment to designing spaces that are accessible, accommodating, and focused on the health and welfare of their user groups.

Commercial
Offices, coworking spaces, lobbies, and communal work environments.

Residential
Single and multi-family units.

Hospitality
Hotels, lounges, and restaurant spaces.

Retail and Entertainment
Retail spaces, emphasis on display and merchandising, movie theaters, bowling alleys.

Educational
K through 12 institutions, spaces for higher education.

Healthcare
Hospitals and clinics. Requires highly qualified expertise.

The Chicbus Alipay flagship store by LYCS Architecture in Hangzhou, China, is a new concept shop for technology products, gadgets and toys. The dynamic pace of product development allows the space to evolve, and function as the backdrop for future product lines and concepts.

Basílica de la Sagrada Família, an unfinished Roman Catholic basilica designed by Antoni Gaudí in Barcelona, Spain, challenges the typical religious institution typology with artfully sculpted detailing and colorful lighting throughout its voluminous space.

96 Unity

The combination of parts that makes a project feel whole.

See Also
Balance
Emphasis
Harmony
Ratio

Unity refers to the combination of all the elements of a design successfully working together in a cohesive way. Although it is often equated with harmony (which means agreement or accord), unity is a separate notion; it is considered the underlying principle that sums up all the cohesive elements of a design project. In an interior, one of the goals of a design is to attempt to bring together the many elements of a project in a coherent and consistent design statement—in other words, to achieve a sense of unity.

There are two types of unity in design

Visual Create unity through the use of contrast, alignment, and repetition. Some examples may include the alignment of elements or the consistent use of color throughout a project.

Conceptual Unify a design by using a specific idea or theme. For example, a project may be framed around a concept of lightness or nature.

However, deploying variety within a unifying composition creates visual and spatial relief, whether it is a unique shape or form, a contrasting color, or varying patterns or textures. Ultimately, a project succeeds when the furniture, lighting, wall treatment, and accessories come together in a unifying way that is pleasing to the user. Unity leads to order and organization, and should ultimately hold together a design visually and conceptually. At key points in the process, designers should take a step back, consult with colleagues, and evaluate the design.

Soft, muted tones, a repeated pattern of decorative wall sconces, furniture, and gold accents, all anchored by a central chandelier, bring unity to this Neoclassical hotel lounge space.

The restaurant of the Villa Copenhagen by in the historic Danish Post and Telegraph Office features green interior spaces that promote a sense of well-being and tranquility in its public areas. The rich, earthy color palette and repeated furniture elements blend together to create a bright, airy space.

The central placement and consistent use of brass detailing, which includes a light fixture, a framed mirror above a fireplace, and a chest of drawers, as well the placement of family heirlooms, come together to unify this living space designed by Cecilia Casagrande in Brookline, Massachusetts.

97 Universal Design

Designing for a diverse range of abilities and situations.

See Also
Accessibility
Design Process
Ergonomics
Inclusivity

Helpful Advice
In 2005, the British Standards Institute defined *inclusive design* as "the design of mainstream products and/or services that are accessible to, and usable by, as many people as reasonably possible . . . without the need for special adaptation or specialized design." Similarly, the expression *universal design* is often used more broadly with emphasis on simplicity, flexibility, and equitability in function.

In the built environment, universal design is the concept that good design should function for all people, disabled or not. The ideas within universal design were first advocated by Ronald Mace, a survivor of polio that left him wheelchair-bound at age ten. He began training as an architect at North Carolina State, where he had to overcome many impediments to moving in and around the campus. His experience led to the development and implementation of principles that are specifically designed to function without the need for customization, adaptation, or specialized equipment to make them accessible. The concept was founded on "eradicating the discrimination, marginalization and social disengagement of the disabled." It is also commonly referred to as design for all, inclusive design, or barrier-free design.

The design solutions that aim to prevent barriers to access tend to feature open, wide spaces that allow movement and circulation, and furniture and fixtures that are accessible, lower to the ground, and require less physical effort to utilize.

The following are key features of the concept of universal design

Flexibility
Ensure that the ease of operation of all elements of a design accommodate people with a broad range of abilities.

Intuitive
Specify fixtures, furniture, and equipment whose function is clear, precise, and operates as expected.

Information
Provide any textual information in a variety of accessible formats, subtitles, high-contrast type, and braille at all locations.

Technology
Approach technology integration with accessibility first by specifying automatic doors, adaptive lighting controlled by sensors, or touch controls that do not need excessive force to operate.

Tactility
Require changes in material at sidewalks and important transitions, and ensure the use of nonslip surfaces.

Helmut Jahn's design for an underground walkway between terminals B and C at O'Hare International Airport in Chicago, Illinois features pedestrian mobility systems that provide ease of movement and circulation for all users of the airport.

Noise-reducing elements, bright colors, and soft surfaces in this office by Ippolito Fleitz Group for the Aktion Mensch headquarters in Bonn, Germany provide clear routes and guidance for all users.

98 Volume

The space within a three-dimensional enclosure.

See Also
Form
Measurement
Shape
Space

Volume is the space contained by four walls, a ceiling, and a floor. When we think of a volume, the first element that comes to mind is a cube; the aggregation of cubes linked by circulation is the definition of an interior environment.

Volumes are defined by planes, and by emphasizing one, or harmonizing all, the designer can utilize the properties of those surfaces to amplify design intent. It is important to recognize the inherent qualities of a volume, as the ratio or proportions of a room affect our senses in many ways.

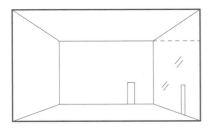

Low Volume
A low volume suggests a more intimate arrangement of furniture and objects. Lower spaces that lead into tall volumes increase the awareness of the change in height.

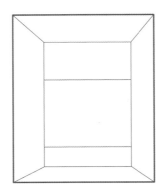

Double- or Multi-Height Volume
Double height, or tall spaces are typically found in civic, retail, and institutional spaces, but sometimes residential projects use such tall spaces.

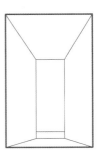

Narrow Volume
Connective volumes, corridors, kitchens, library stacks, and stairwells are all examples. These spaces typically enclose functional elements, make adjacencies possible, and may be considered secondary spaces.

The Remai Modern museum, designed by KPMB in Saskatoon, Saskatchewan, volumes are used as both an exterior organizing strategy, and an interior space for circulation and connection.

99 Wayfinding

The use of visual information systems to guide people through an environment.

See Also

Accessibility
Codes
Health, Safety,
 and Welfare
Inclusivity

The idea of wayfinding was developed in Cambridge, Massachusetts. The urbanist Kevin Lynch in his book *The Image of the City* outlines five key elements that enables people in a city to legibly find their destination paths, edges, districts, nodes, and landmarks. Interiors of museums, offices, educational buildings, and healthcare and transportation facilities need visual systems that aid in navigating these complex spaces so that users can find their destination.

Maps, symbols and icons, large-scale graphics and directories form the basis of a wayfinding system, which is developed through a series of interviews, user scenarios, and mock-ups to determine a family of signs and place-making elements. Increasingly, the use of non-textual and touch-based elements are being used to address issues of accessibility and access.

Wayfinding systems can be playful and integral to the interior design of a space, and complement decisions about finish and color, while at the same time provide necessary information about use, occupancy, and egress.

Further Reading

The Society for Experiential Graphic Design, "What Is Wayfinding?," segd.org/what-wayfinding.

M.R. O'Connor, *Wayfinding The Science and Mystery of How Humans Navigate the World* (St. Martin's Press, 2019).

Although Kevin Lynch's paths, edges, districts, nodes, and landmarks reference the exterior environment, his ideas hold true for interior spaces.

The Calgary Library by Snøhetta features signage by Entro that reflects the building's design.

Follow That Food
Dig Into Nature

Play With Me

Make Your Mark
Move With The River

Restrooms

Vertical wayfinding signs are typical in museum spaces, and can add a snap of color, as seen in the Louisiana Children's Museum in New Orleans by Studio Matthews, or appear more muted, as in MIT's Department of Urban Studies and Planning in Cambridge, Massachusetts, by OverUnder.

100 Zones

The separation of areas of a space according to their function.

See Also
Circulation
Connection
Program
Space

A part of the programming phase of a project, the development of zones helps indicate the main areas of a design to begin space planning, indicate their relative area and adjacency, and begin the process of determining levels of privacy, environmental quality, and technical need.

The placement of zones is also influenced by their location in a building, the orientation to sun paths, adjacency requirements, and path of travel. A careful zoning study will reveal the placement and range between enclosed and open spaces. Zones can be expanded by the use of overlapping of function; for instance, open-office planning can have spaces that provide for multiple functions.

In a residential project, zones are prescribed by the level of activity and interaction. These are typically formed around social needs, private space, work needs, and storage. In addition, space should be reserved for circulation.

In commercial spaces, space planning is used as a complement to zoning. It examines the needs of an organization that has to budget for both human resources and furniture, fixture, and equipment (FF&E) requirements.

Knoll's "Immersive Planning" study (2016) illustrates how the floorplan of an office demonstrates the fluid overlap of zones in a workspace.

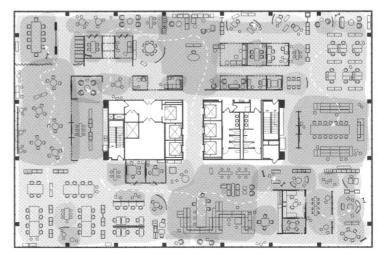

The Grid, a system
by Ronan and Erwan
Bouroullec for
Established & Sons, is
playfully used to establish
residential areas.

The different zones of
The Ace Hotel lobby in
Kyoto by Kengo Kuma &
Associates with interiors
by Commune Design are
indicated through the
use of texture, furniture,
and light.

Universal Principles of Interior Design

Acknowledgments

We were approached and began to write this book in the middle of a pandemic, in the middle of online school for our two kids, and trying to maintain three businesses, in which our personal and professional lives are intertwined—architecture, design, furniture, and education. We were also learning new languages for PPP loans, grants and stop-gap measures to keep everything afloat.

The call to write this book arrived at a time when uncertainties about the future was in constant flux, when struggles against racism and representation brought our own inadequacies to the forefront of thought, and in a pivotal moment when the future of the country we live in was in question, when we were kept awake at night wondering if we needed to flee north or even further away.

With this writing, research, and documentation of this book, we have tried to represent the world of interior design as comprehensively as possible, and to reframe the western-centric histories and examples that we were taught in school, and have written about in the past. These processes are emergent, and as such, we fully accept our shortcomings here. We wish we had more time, more energy, and more resources to reference, and we hope that some of our work begins to correct that record.

Our continued thanks to the following their input and insight when we were attempting to figure out the most relevant principles to include Dorothy Deak, Megan Dobstaff, Brian Graham, Royce Epstein, Peter Grimley, Jessica Klein, Sarah Kuchar, Virginia Schubert, Sascha Wagner.

Much gratitude for the many hands and eyes that have helped us on the book. The persistence and organization by Josie Cerbone, who took on the daunting task of co-ordinating images and rights, the early research efforts of Margaret Robe, and the team at Rockport/Quarto—Joy Aquilino, David Martinell, and John Gettings. We are indebted to our proofreader, Martha Wetherill, who took our words and elevated them to prose. Any remaining mistakes are our responsibility.

Thanks to the designers, architects and photographers, that allowed us to share their work. The inclusion of your labor and talent enriches our attempt to quantify what is a constantly changing and evolving profession.

Finally, this book would not have been possible without a decision a young man made in Glasgow, Scotland, sixty years ago. He was advised to finish apprenticing as a sign-painter, and to go to the Strathclyde School of Building to train as an Interior Designer. He left the United Kingdom as a young man to pursue his dreams, and moved, sight unseen, to Canada to continue a career in what was then an emerging profession. This courage (to leave England when he had a son that was only 6 months old), led to the establishment of his own independent design office, which at the time was struggling to assert itself against the disparaging efforts of the 'architects' in the room to assert itself as a viable, and legitimate, profession. His son followed him to offices and job sites, went to school to earn a degree in the same discipline. We dedicate this book to Peter Grimley—Interior Designer, ARIDO President Emeritus, Glasgow Celtic supporter, father.

Index

Credits

The authors and publishers have made every reasonable effort to contact all persons or organizations with a copyright claim on the works published herein. Every effort has been made to ensure accuracy at the time of printing and any corrections will be made in future editions, provided notice is given to the publisher.

All drawings, images and screenshots by OverUnder unless otherwise noted.

Authors

Chris Grimley has organized, designed, and implemented experiential environments, interiors, master plans, and branding initiatives for clients ranging from small offices to large institutions. He has broad experience in architecture, graphic design, and interior design. He is the co-author and designer of several books, including *The Interior Design Reference & Specification Book* (2018), *Imagining the Modern Architecture and Urbanism of the Pittsburgh Renaissance* (2019), and *Heroic Concrete Architecture and the New Boston* (2015). Recognition and awards include those from AIGA, SEGD, HOW, docomomo, the Boston Preservation Alliance and the Boston Society of Architects. He lives in Boston, Massachusetts.

Kelly Harris Smith is a designer, creative director, and entrepreneur specializing in natural and sustainable materials for commercial and residential interior design. A co-founder of FilzFelt (acquired by Knoll, Inc. in 2011), Kelly's award-winning designs are distinctive for their pattern, color, and innovative functionality. Kelly is also the founder of Minni, a community creative space in Boston offering art and design education to young children. She was awarded Product Designer Award at Interior Design's HiP 2020 and Emerging Product Designer Award at NYCxDesign in 2018. She trained in architecture at Northeastern University and resides in Boston, Massachusetts.